101.9

UNIST★R

LEADING
the
WAY

RK

FIDELIS CARE

CW00631879

business

graphics

mike quon

& graphic design:usa

 PBC International, Inc.

To my family, for all their support

Distributor to the book trade in the United States and Canada
Rizzoli International Publications Inc.
300 Park Avenue South
New York, NY 10010

Distributor to the art trade in the United States and Canada
PBC International, Inc.
One School Street
Glen Cove, NY 11542

Distributor throughout the rest of the world
Hearst Books International
1350 Avenue of the Americas
New York, NY 10019

Copyright © 1995 by
PBC INTERNATIONAL, INC.
All rights reserved. No part of this book may be
reproduced in any form whatsoever without
written permission of the copyright owner,
PBC INTERNATIONAL, INC.
One School Street, Glen Cove, NY 11542.

Library of Congress Cataloging–in–Publication Data

Business Graphics / by Mike Quon and Graphic Design:usa
        p.   cm.
     Includes index.
     ISBN 0–86636–389–0   (pbk ISBN 0–86636–391–2)
     1. Commercial art. 2. Graphic arts. I. Graphic Design:usa
(Firm) II. Title.
NC998.4.Q66 1995   94–22628
741.6—dc20   CIP

CAVEAT– Information in this text is believed accurate, and will pose no problem for the student or casual reader.
However, the author was often constrained by information contained in signed release forms, information that could
have been in error or not included at all. Any misinformation (or lack of information) is the result of failure in these
attestations. The author has done whatever is possible to insure accuracy.

Color separation by Fine Arts Repro House Co., Ltd., H. K.
Printing and binding by Toppan Printing Co., H. K.

Photography by Naum Kazhdan, 58 Third Street, Brooklyn, NY 11218 unless otherwise noted.

10 9 8 7 6 5 4 3 2 1

Printed in Hong Kong

contents

Foreword

aubrey balkind, ceo
frankfurt balkind partners

Overload. Overload. We are buried daily by more information than we can process. How do we cope with this barrage? Instead of processing much of the information, we make messages disappear; we simply don't see them or hear them; we zap TV commercials, we toss out mail unopened; or we take only a bite out of any whole piece.

Audiences no longer categorize these competing bits of information, giving each its own share of attention. Now corporate communications, daily newspapers, monthly magazines and TV shows wage war on the same playing field for our limited attention.

So how can corporate communications meet this challenge?

To convey their message, corporations must fight the competition with their own weapons, fusing entertainment with substance. After all, the most successful communicator in our society is the entertainment industry. From it we need to learn how to involve and, yes, seduce our audiences.

Corporate communications must talk in a voice and style that shuns "corporatese," that actually *says* something and says it clearly. All too often, companies haven't quite worked out what they want to say; they use buzz words to obfuscate their messages, and they leave readers staring blankly at the end of a sentence. Today's readers move on...fast.

We must remember that corporate communications always speaks to *people*, whether they are security analysts, employees, or governments. They are people first, and they respond powerfully to emotional appeals, not just rational messages. Humor, whimsy, pathos...used appropriately, make a corporate message more human so that it is absorbed, internalized and remembered.

Designers must become communicators. Design cannot concern itself solely with layout or decoration. It first has to get involved with the concept and then make the text work harder to deliver its message. It must entice people onto the page and be structured so that today's skimming readers can enter a document at any point and understand how that piece fits into the whole. And all this must be driven by a corporate strategy that is understandable, meaningful and compelling to the company's diverse audiences.

All this is a tall task. Designers who create true communications are critically important contributors to a corporation's success.

Preface

gordon d. kaye, co-publisher/editor . graphic design:usa

As editor and publisher of the monthly national news magazine, *Graphic Design: usa*, I wanted—fully, enthusiastically, energetically—to be involved in this *Business Graphics* project.

I believe this is an important book for two reasons.
The first reason is that graphic design is coming of age as a discipline because the best practitioners of it are increasingly market driven and marketing savvy, and because corporate and institutional clients have come to recognize that design is not merely a frill or a decoration, but an integral part of (a) the planning, development, and marketing of products and services, and (b) the projection of a corporate image and attitude that can transcend the information overload we all live with.

This phenomenon—this marriage of design and marketing, if you will—has been latecoming to corporate literature because of its past tendency to take the safe, predictable, repetitive route. But, in our editorial staff's opinion (*Graphic Design: usa* reviews more annual reports and corporate literature than anyone, anywhere), the floodgates have opened and, arguably, the best, smartest, most targeted corporate graphics work ever done is being done right now. As the selections in this book demonstrate, the "marriage" is bearing fruit, resulting in powerful and directed communications in support of corporate needs, policies and goals.

The second reason this book is important is that it will help set straight a nascent misconception. There is a "buzz" these days that the deep penetration of the computer into graphic design—and the paving of the information superhighway—is making design-for-print an increasingly irrelevant backwater.

This does not reflect reality. It is true that the Macintosh is dramatically changing the role of the creator of artwork—placing designers in the center of the creative and production processes, and allowing easier preparation of art and information for a variety of media output such as multimedia, video, interactive, CD-ROM. But to conclude that print will not be an important—indeed, the dominant—medium well into the next millennium for business and corporate communications is a "techie" pipe dream, unsupported by fact, by experience, by common sense, or by human nature. Each of these digital mediums is finding limited, niche uses, but none seriously threatens the broad-based, easy accessibility, user-friendly relevance of print. And, in almost every case, literature complements or coexists with these other pieces.

Print will continue to be the staple for most projects and the staple for most working graphic designers for as far as the eye can see.

Likewise, it is just plain wrong to conclude that the availability of digital delivery suddenly and inherently renders ink-on-paper impotent. As the bold, innovative, exciting, stimulating works shown in this book make clear, corporate literature can be as imaginative as the mind of a great designer. Mark Twain in his prime, upon learning that he had been referred to in a newspaper article as "the late Mark Twain," retorted that "reports of my demise are greatly exaggerated." One need only explore *Business Graphics* to know—intellectually and emotionally—that reports of print's demise are similarly greatly exaggerated.

"Business

is too

important

to be

left to

businessmen."

john kenneth galbraith

Introduction

From the moment the morning news begins, we're

bombarded by corporate design and promotion.

It's telecast from the 30-second TV spot, shines from the

pages of glossy brochures and magazines, jumps off our

mail, attaches itself to packages and shouts from billboards.

As the information superhighway clamors more and more

for our attention — so will high-tech corporate graphics.

In the looming visual landscape of printed materials, it is

increasingly important for businesses to distinguish

themselves from their competition.

b Corporate design is working harder than ever before, with more innovation and persuasion, to reach visually inundated and discriminating audiences – to inform, entertain and impress.

Business Graphics takes a look at some of today's best design in corporate literature – brochures, annual reports, sales literature and collateral *(promotional material)* – to show how this traditionally conservative arena of communications is breaking old rules of design and growing modern. Many designers are pushing their corporate clients past clichés and toward the cutting edge. Even the most conservative industries, such as investment firms and insurance companies, are experimenting with new design ideas to reach their more diversified audience. The Black & Decker Corporation, among others, has realized the potential of cool, clean design to further enhance its status in the corporate world.

The corporate client demands more than just a pleasing and reassuring image. They are looking to the graphic

"...the tendency

to become safe,

overly conservative,

and to analyze every

situation takes the

spontaneity out of the

design process.

It's hard to lead when

you're looking over

your shoulder."

ron dumas

Nike

> **"Imagination is more important than knowledge."**
>
> **Albert Einstein**

designer to play a larger role in selling a product, service or image. They want more than just a photograph of a CEO. They are looking to the designer for marketing, technical and high-impact graphic support – to produce compelling corporate literature. It has an important job to do, and it has to do it in a matter of seconds. The material must involve the reader. It lets us know through images just who the company is. We can be struck by the sense of confidence of a brochure or annual report. In today's competitive environment, each piece must have impact. If a brochure doesn't immediately grab the reader, it will not be read.

Bold, daring artwork, powerful photography, unique graphics and clever editorial join in stimulating corporate design. Design is supposed to be beyond style, but the short-lived nature of print graphics makes them especially vulnerable to trends and fads. There seems to be no one corporate style. The trend is toward complete freedom. In the current

Elbert Hubbard (early public relations wizard)

"The man who does not advertise is a dead one, whether he knows it or not. Life is too short for you to hide yourself away mantled in your own modesty."

market, designers make use of new technology to create

images that are more visually active than ever before, and

are literally 'in your face' or 'over your head.' Corporations

are also keeping their designs looking human, neither too

highly technical nor sterile. The new technologies in

computer graphics are the hallmark of this new design,

blending art and photography, stretching, mutating,

reorganizing information to create fresh looks. The

computer-illustrative approach shown in Time Warner's

annual report is a fine example of technology leading style

without losing reason or intent. Graphic design has also

been crossing over to a fine arts orientation: fine and

commercial arts together, once thought incompatible.

This commingling of mediums lets designers introduce new

solutions to familiar problems. In choosing bold expressive

illustrations the Potlach/Kvester Group gave themselves a

fresh angle of attack over their competitors.

Technology and a new computer aesthetic can take much of

the credit for the changing attitudes in corporate design.

These changes are helping to make the old conservative

André Maurois

"Business is a combination of war and sport.

BELIEVE.

It's been said that the heaviest burdens
are placed upon the strongest shoulders.
If that's so, then believing in yourself
is surely the purest source of strength.
At Great Country Bank,
we never underestimate the power of believing.
In ourselves. Our customers. And in tomorrow.
It has the potential not only to crumble obstacles,
but to triumph amidst raging winds of change.

GREAT COUNTRY
BANK
The Bank That Believes
Member FDIC

TRUST.

In a world of broken hearts, trust is a circle.
The surest way to gain it is to give it away.
With out trust, the spirit has no wings.
There its need, and what grows is
the most powerful bond between human beings.
At Great Country Bank, we placed your trust
in our most valuable asset.
And in times of prosperity or uncertainty,
you can always count on us.

GREAT COUNTRY
BANK
The Bank That Believes
Member FDIC

FAITH.

Like a bird in the rain,
then faith is surely the mortar
that holds them together.
Having a little faith is the leaping moment all.
In trying times, it has the power
not just critical, but to inspire.
At Great Country Bank,
Faith is what we're all about.
Faith in our customers,
In the strength of our community,
Faith in a stronger tomorrow.

GREAT COUNTRY
BANK
The Bank That Believes
Member FDIC

"The problem with most corporate design

today is that it's too corporate."

cheryl heller

Frankfurt Balkind Partners

"Designers imitate designers.

Corporations imitate corporations.

It's easy, comfortable, and safe.

I wish all of us could be more original."

stephen frykholm

Herman Miller

"Among designers, too much time is spent

talking about technology when technology is

just a tool for producing concepts. We are

designers and our focus needs to be on

design and on educating people outside the

profession on design values."

steve liska

Liska & Associates

"Design that effectively communicates will eliminate frills, contrivances and extraneous material, instead of adding these nonessentials. If your core idea is a good one, the idea will shout loudest when it's not buried by, strewn with or overwhelmed by ornamentation."

roger cook

Cook & Shanosky

"The merchant in the 21st century will be more of a showman than he is today, more creative, more innovative, more concerned with how he presents his message to his customer."

david l. yunich

"It's time for me to be on my way, I know, I've got business to conduct and places to go..."

billy joel

Temptation

standards of the traditional design process obsolete.
The computer empowers a designer to create images that
would have been prohibitive in both time and expense.

The examples in this book are visually arresting, stimulating
and successful at communicating a corporate message.
Whether it is the sophistication of the Engelhard
Corporation, the starkness of Converse or the cool style

of Nike, each approach is appropriate and successful in
communicating its individual message. I picked these pieces
because they effectively define and illustrate a company's
service or product; they convey an identity/image with high
quality and graphics, and balanced meaty editorial.

As the corporate culture changes, so does the graphic look
of design. It's constantly changing, moving into new
territory — corporate robo chic. Who would have thought
that teenage computer nerds working in their garages
would come up with stuff so highly sought after by today's
corporate designers?

We're loosening our ties, unbuttoning our collars, breaking
rules and pushing the limits. Hang on, the great corporate
graphics adventure continues, and the best is yet to come.

– Mike Quon

Thou shalt not steal

Exod. 20:15

brochures

client
repap
design firm
castagne communications inc.
art director
robert demougeot
illustrator
lee dunnette
photographer
serge hambourg

client
simpson paper company
design firm
pentagram design inc.
designers
kit hinrichs   belle how
amy chan
mask artists
mcray magleby   james cross
kit hinrichs   gerald reis
dan picasso   heinz edelmann

Simpson's recycling program is dedicated to proving that premium text and cover papers can be made from waste fibers without sacrificing print quality and fine design. Our success is apparent in Gainsborough, Coronado SST Recycled and Sundance, well-established grades that are now recycled, and in other popular recycled grades like Quest, EverGreen, and new Equinox which have become recognized for their high waste-fiber content and aesthetic appeal. For Simpson, recycling challenges innovation.

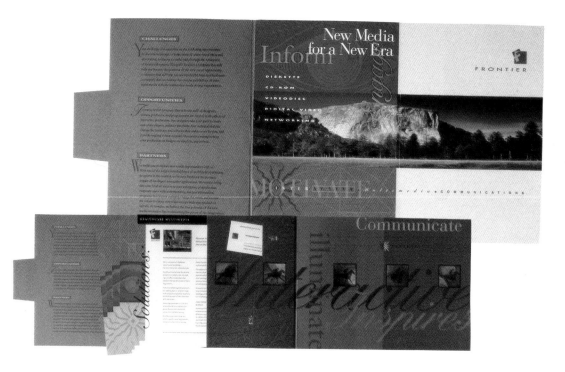

client
frontier media group, inc.
design firm
bjornson design associates inc.
art director/illustrator
jon anders bjornson
photography
courtesy of fpg international *cover*

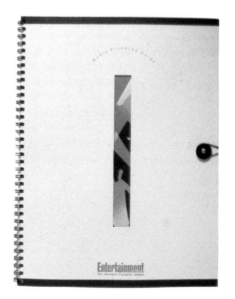

client
entertainment weekly
design firm
platinum
art directors
vickie peslak
sandra quinn
designer
sandra quinn

client
ids (interior design services)
design firm
winner koenig & associates
creative director
joni spencer
designer
julie davis
photographer
gary resnick

client
nichols institute
design firm
jann church partners, inc.
designer
jann church

technology
assessment
group

MISSION

Our mission is
to facilitate reasoned thinking
on the long range impact
of future technologies
and promote creation of plans
to exploit their development.

APPROACH

Our approach
is a three-phased process for
articulating alternative futures and
planning appropriate actions.

EXPLOITING TOMORROW'S TECHNOLOGY

ANDERSEN CONSULTING

client
andersen consulting
design firm
mark oldach design
art director
mark oldach
designer
don emery

TECHNOLOGY [T] ASSESSMENT

EXPLOITING TOMORROW'S TECHNOLOGY

ANDERSEN CONSULTING

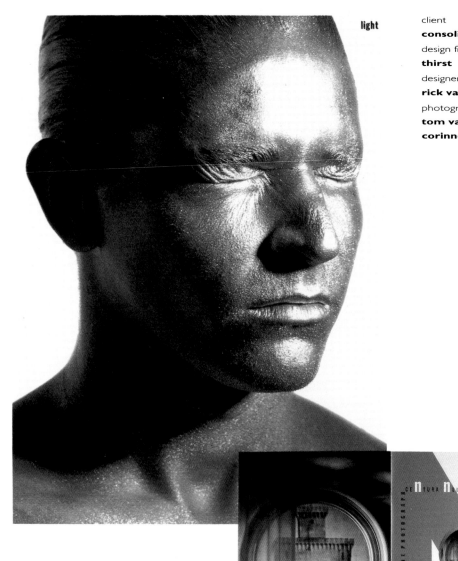

light

client
consolidated papers, inc.
design firm
thirst
designer
rick valicenti
photographers
tom vack
corinne pfister

CENTURA NEITHER WARM NOR COLD THIS COLOR-BALANCED WHITE

INTENT OF THE PHOTOGRAPH NEVER INTERFERES WITH THE ORIGINAL

CENTURA
TRUE FIDELITY
IN COLOR AND TONE
TO THE ORIGINAL ART

client
repap
design firm
castagne communications inc.
art director
robert demougeot

4

NATURAL FORMS

bring a sense of HARMONY.

to their surroundings.

The end result, Beauty.

client
suncraft mills
design firm
images design
designers
lisa beichrath
photographer
neal farris

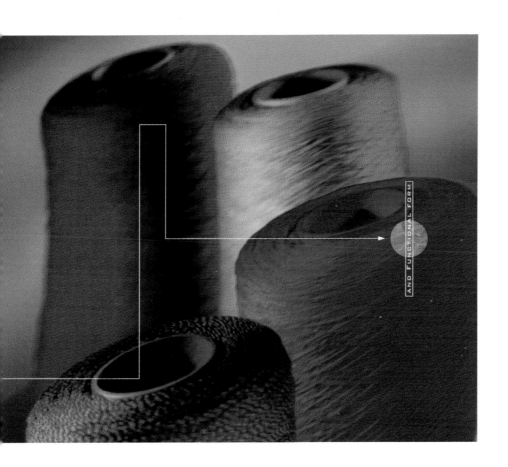

AND FUNCTIONAL FORM

THE subtle POWER OF NATURE AND THE BEAUTY OF ITS enduring DESIGN. THE epitome OF CLASSIC DESIGN: COLOR, TEXTURE AND PATTERN COMBINED IN A natural SETTING.

client
gilbert paper
design firm
worksight
art director/designer
scott w. santoro
photographer
lon murdick

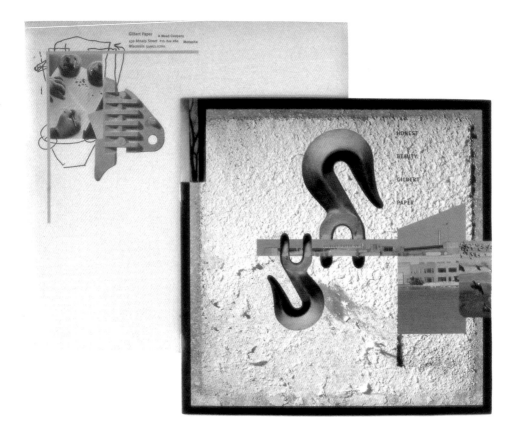

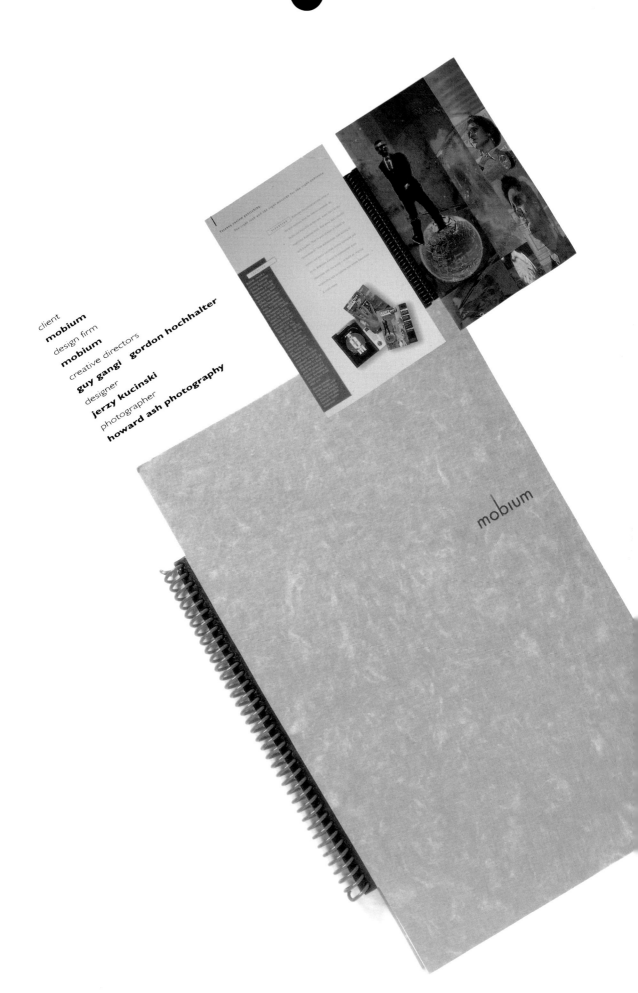

client
mobium
design firm
mobium
creative directors
guy gangi   gordon hochhalter
designer
jerzy kucinski
photographer
howard ash photography

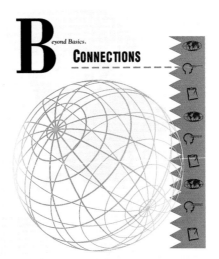

client
mcgraw-hill inc.
design firm
chris gorman associates, inc.
art director/designer
chris gorman

client
greenfield/belser ltd.
design firm
greenfield/belser ltd.
art director
burkey belser
designers
burkey belser   joe kayser
erika ritzer   john lineberger
linda santopietro
photography
john burwell   stock photography

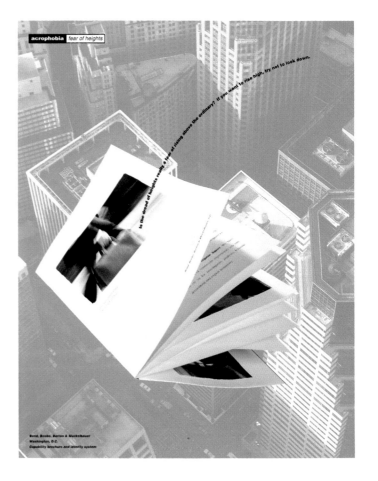

Set a new standard of excellence for your industry.

Responsive service strategies, including partnership initiatives, require that you share vital information and align business practices with customers and suppliers. With PROCESS/1 you can deliver quality service tailored to each unique relationship.

Order Management

Add value. Speed products to customers. Ensure satisfaction.

PROCESS/1 flexibility lets you centralize order entry and distribute order fulfillment, with improved productivity and accuracy throughout the process.

Streamlines Order Entry

• EDI order acceptance and confirmation

• Full range of order types, including quotes, customer-specific contracts and future orders

• Automatic pricing, promotions, credit checking and tax calculations

• Checks product restrictions

• Automatic item substitutions

Reliable Delivery Scheduling

• Automatic inventory availability checking and allocation

• Network-wide sourcing

• Production pipeline visibility and reservation

• Lot reservation to meet specific customer requirements

Pricing an

Increase ma
product-li
administ

PROC
unsu
hel
im

Enables International Trading

• Multicurrency and multilanguag

• Export documentation

• Value-added taxes (VAT)

• EC inter-company trading

PROCESS/1

The Software
Solution for Food
and Consumer
Packaged Goods
Manufacturers.

Free Exchange of Information

ANDERSEN
CONSULTING
Software Products

client
andersen consulting
design firm
tanagram, inc.
designers
anthony ma   lance rutter

client
the merchandise mart chicago
design firm
segura inc.
designer
carlos segura
photographer
geof kern

client
southern california edison
design firm
maureen erbe design
art director
maureen erbe
designers
maureen erbe   rita sowins
illustrator
pearl beach

client
acs (affiliated computer systems)
design firm
sibley/peteet design, inc.
art director/designer
rex peteet
illustrator
julia albanesi
photographer
klein & wilson

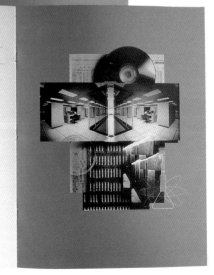

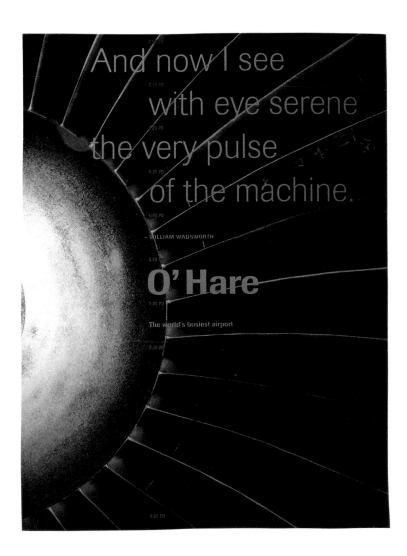

And now I see
with eye serene
the very pulse
of the machine.

— WILLIAM WADSWORTH

O'Hare

The world's busiest airport

client
consolidated papers, inc.

design firm
liska and associates, inc.

art director
steve liska

designer
valerie cote

photographer
tim bieber

the FUTURE
belongs to
THOSE WITH the
vision
to see it

The future also belo
with the vision to

A Survey of
AND
BUILDS FOR GRAND
WITH MODERN METHO
the WORLD
Exposition ore profitable for you!
FURNIS ON workplace ...corporate
DESIGN FOR IT A WORLD FOCUS planning and
DIE WE DESIGN
future
BEST-QUALT
World Le Monde World
THINKING. concepts
MODULARS in the right place
GRAND BUSINESS at the right time
ROUNDUP

THE MERCHANDISE MART

PAID

address correction requested

The world is changing shape.
Is your thinking changing with

THE WORLD IS SHAPING UP TO BE A RATHER CHALLENGING PLACE. TODAY, YOU MUST CREATE A WORK ENVIRON
COMPANY'S IMMEDIATE NEEDS WHILE MAINTAINING FLEXIBILITY FOR THE FUTURE. A FUTURE IN WHICH THE
ACCELERATED TECHNOLOGICAL CHANGE, A GROWING LABOR SHORTAGE AND NEW
ORGANIZATIONAL STRUCTURES WILL BE INCREASINGLY
CRITICAL FACTORS FOR SUCCESS. WHICH IS WHY
NeoCon'92 IS VITAL TO YOUR COMPANY. AT NeoCon,
YOU'LL DISCOVER THE LATEST IDEAS IN WORKPLACE
PLANNING AND DESIGN. YOU'LL SEE THE NEWEST
PRODUCTS FROM THE WORLD'S LEADING CONTRACT
FURNISHINGS MANUFACTURERS. YOU'LL LEARN NEW
DESIGN SOLUTIONS IN OVER 60 AREA EDUCATIONAL
SEMINARS AND WORKSHOPS TO HELP CREATE A MORE
PRODUCTIVE WORKPLACE FOR YOUR COMPANY. NOW AND IN YEARS TO COME.

Attend
and keep success i

NeoCon92 A remarkable opportunity to create a workplace that works in an ever changing

to CREATE A
more productive
WORKPLACE, see
things
from A new
PERSPECTIVE

AND
BUILDS F
FUR
THINK

NeoCon92
THE WORLD EXPOSITION ON WORKPLACE PLANNING & DESIGN

Imagine the
designed with

register now

Thrive

THE FUTURE OF WORKPLACE PLA

furnish your mind.

client
the merchandise mart chicago
design firm
segura inc.
designer
carlos segura
photographer
geof kern

NeoCon usa
The Merchandise Mart ◦ Chicago, Illinois 60654

the FUTURE belongs to THOSE WITH the *vision* to see it

NeoCon92

to CREATE A more productive WORKPLACE, see

from A new PERSPECTIVE

The future belongs to those with the vision to plan ahead.

This year, attending NeoCon has never been easier. For one thing, NeoCon is *free*. For another, travel and accommodations have never been more affordable. Because The Merchandise Mart proudly introduces the Mart Center Travel Service. With one toll-free telephone call, you can reserve and confirm all airline, car rental and

NEOCON92 • JUNE 8th THRU 10th • AT THE MERCHANDISE MART OF CHICAGO

other travel arrangements, as well as hotel accommodations. Of course, you can register for NeoCon92 at the same time. Using *the mart center travel service* guarantees you the lowest applicable airfares at the time of your phone call. If airfares are lowered after you have made your reservations, and you qualify for the lower fare, the savings will be passed on to you.

In addition, many hotels will be offering double occupancy at single room rates, so you can share a room and the expense with an associate. Rates will be as low as $42.50 each for an $85 hotel room making the new Mart Center Travel Service an opportunity to plan ahead that should not be cast aside. If you do not need travel arrangements, you can register for NeoCon — or receive more information — by calling NeoCon at 800.677.6278.

MAKE YOUR TRAVEL ARRANGEMENTS FOR NEOCON92 TODAY.
BY CALLING TOLL FREE 800.528.8700   *furnish your mind.*

this is your   *last chance to*

FACE THE FUTURE

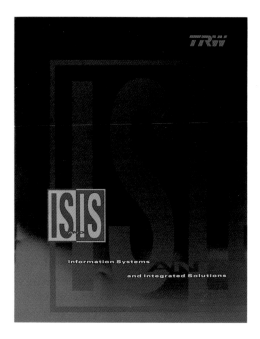

client
trw systems integration group
design firm
trw systems integration group
art director
randall fung
photographers
lawrence manning
randall fung

Crowded prisons. Welfare abuse. Tax delinquency. Emergency management. Rapid growth and shrinking budgets. These are the difficult problems facing state and local governments. State, county and city agencies must each deal with a multitude of issues while grappling with ever-dwindling resources. How can governments meet these challenges and still stay within budget?

At TRW, high technology doesn't mean high cost. Utilizing open systems architectures, integrated computer-aided software engineering tools, relational databases with 4th Generation Languages, and data integration/migration techniques, our ISIS specialists can reduce the cost, development, and implementation time of client/server information systems by orders of magnitude. We have a proven track record of integrating large client/server architectures, local- and wide-area networks, database management systems, and imaging systems. We apply these technologies to office automation records and case management, document processing, electronic commerce, and other applications.

Whether it's a system for prison management, automated welfare, electronic tax filing, emergency dispatch, or other functions, TRW has the experience and tools necessary for prompt, effective solutions to the problems of state and local governments.

client
ntvic
design firm
mike quon design office, inc.
creative director
mike quon
designers
sam gunn   eileen kinneary

NTVIC

WHEN YOU'RE
BROADCASTING
TO THE WORLD

NTV INTERNATIONAL CORPORATION

client
entertainment weekly
design firm
platinum
art directors
vickie peslak
sandra quinn
designer
sandra quinn

client
lasertechnics, inc.
design firm
vaughn wedeen creative
art director/designer
steve wedeen
photographer
michael barley

client
dayton hudson
design firm
nike design
art director/designer
john norman
photographer
gary hush

No Boundaries Tee 100% cotton jersey T-shirt.

Color-blocked Crinkle Short 100% nylon short with a mesh liner and side-seam pockets.

Air Trainer Vengeance Low & stable, well-cushioned cross trainer for the versatile athlete.

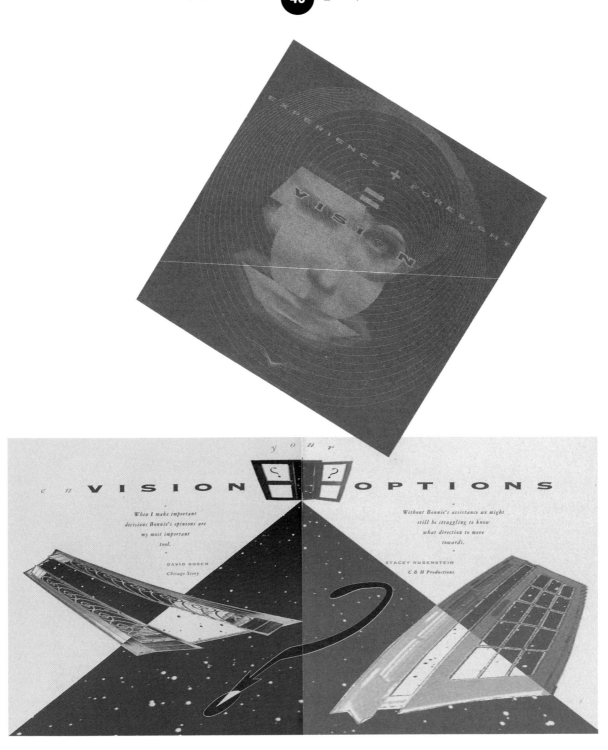

client
the deems consultancy
design firm
tanagram, inc.
designer
anthony ma
illustrators/photographers
eric wagner   michael bom

client
woven legends restoration inc.
design firm
bjornson design associates inc.
art director
john anders bjornson
photographer
gary mckinnis

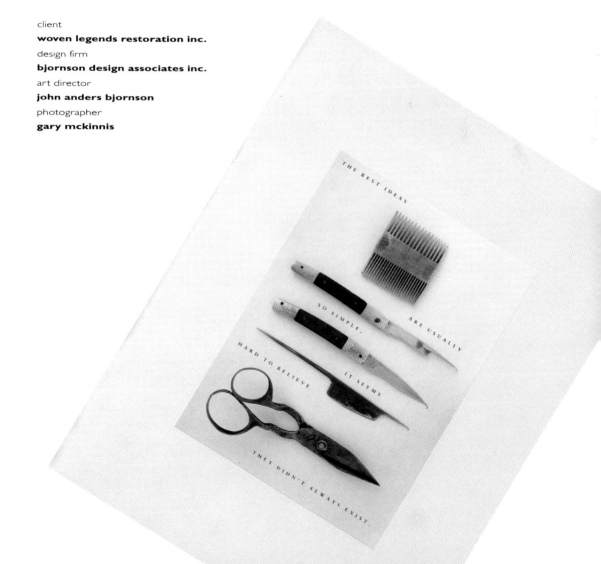

Today's lease terms must incorporate the flexibility to accommodate any corporate action—both planned and unforeseen. Our dynamic business environment demands it. Strong, skilled tenant representation counsel can assist you in anticipating the unique facility needs of your business now and in the future.

Whether your property is held for long-term appreciation or sold for development, the resulting transaction requires a thorough knowledge—and continued monitoring—of the marketplace and demographic trends.

Your relationship with building management is critical, and often represents your only contact with building ownership. As a tenant, you expect to receive the services called for in the lease agreement.

Building management maintains responsibility to deliver these services. As a safeguard, your representation counsel should be willing to interact with ownership will after occupancy.

"Location, location, location." This adage about the three most desirable real estate attributes is equally applicable to your leased office space. Proximity to major arterials, airports, amenities and financial centers still influences most tenant's geographic decisions.

Your business expense budget for office and other facility needs is significant, typically second only to payroll. Negotiated concessions—to cost move-ins, discounts for extended lease periods, over-standard tenant improvements, restrictions on excessive cost pass-throughs—can mean significant savings to a key expense category.

Your building's electrical and telecommunication capacities should be sufficient to accommodate long-term corporate growth. Similarly, physical space expansion needs covered under first right of refusal, must-take and other option clauses must be considered in advance.

Renewal terms, subleasing, assignment, operating cost calculations, and options need to be thoroughly understood—and vigorously negotiated.

Amenities are more than attractive work environment features—they have become integral to recruitment and retention of quality employees. Location of child care services, health club facilities, basement and professional organizations, restaurants and security issues should be factored into space decision-making.

MERIDIAN PACIFIC
Commercial Real Estate Brokerage/Consulting

Office space requirements are as uniquely different as square pegs and round holes.

client
meridian pacific
design firm
white design
art director/designer
john white
illustrator
neil shigley

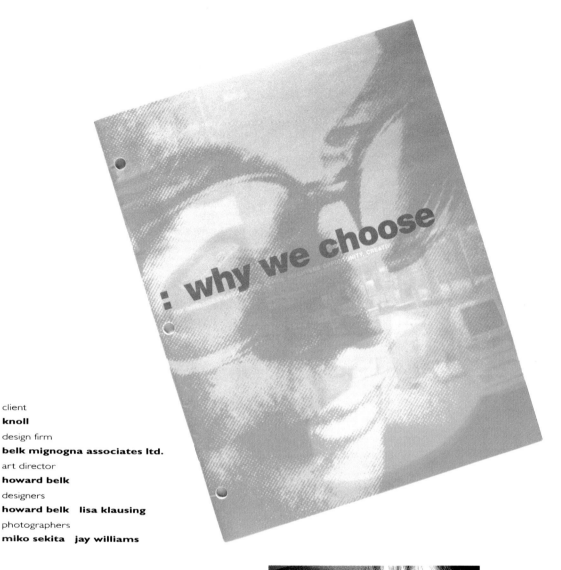

: why we choose

client
knoll

design firm
belk mignogna associates ltd.

art director
howard belk

designers
howard belk   lisa klausing

photographers
miko sekita   jay williams

In a world where change is a given, any solution for planning and furnishing an office means thinking ahead. Morrison Network's superbly engineered, interchangeable freestanding and panel-supported components create the feel of permanence, yet provide the capacity for reconfiguring an office overnight. And Knoll Group dealers are there to help.

a **facilities manager's** *view*

AS IT'S SYSTEMATICALLY ADAPTED, THE WORKSPACE EMPOWERS THE END USER TO PERFORM THE VARIOUS FUNCTIONS WHICH DETERMINE ITS FINAL SHAPE.

"Planning for change is built into Morrison Network. We can create open plan workstations as well as private offices."

solutions

and service

client
international paper company
design firm
oden & associates
creative director
bret terwilleger
art director
collins dillard
illustrator
vineet thapar
photographers
phillip parker   allen mims
russell comfort   jim ramer
glen phillips

client
clairol, inc.

design firm
mike quon design office, inc.

creative directors
mike quon
scott fishoff

designer
eileen kinneary

ARCHITEXTURE®

PERMANENT WAVING SYSTEM

FOR NATURAL HAIR   FOR TINTED HAIR

THE ULTIMATE FOUNDATION FOR PERFECT PERMING:

1 BUILD ON A FIRM BASE

An acid wave with versatility...the perm today's trendsetters want. Architexture delivers thick, voluminous waves with the long-lasting advantage of an alkaline perm. Lots you create hi-fashion, multi-designs on all hair types and textures—bring fine delicate hair to new heights.

Architexture also lets you control results. It's fortified with rich conditioners and firming ingredients, so curls stay consistent throughout the life of the perm. And, it's pH-controlled for quick and easy processing.

2 ADD SHAPE, STRUCTURE AND FORM.

Architexture towers high above other acid-balanced perms. Its unique Curl Structurizers put it there. You'll see curl strength and resilience, elasticity...no fear of fragile curls. You'll get soft, springy texture... predictable, true-to-rod size results.

3 KEEP THE PROCESS EVEN

There's no dryer heat needed with Architexture ...it processes with gentle body heat. There's no client discomfort, no uneven curl formation.

4 POLISH TO PERFECTION.

Architexture has a Cationic Conditioning System built into the perm lotion and neutralizer. It therefore works throughout the entire perm process—and actually lets you see its effectiveness in action. It foams up as its positive cationic charges bond to hair's negative ones. It is most active during processing when hair is at its weakest chemical state—when its cystine bonds are broken. The result is a perm that's softer, shinier, better conditioned after perming than before.

5 GIVE IT AN EXTRA EDGE.

Architexture gives you more for your clients... it's easy to maintain, delivers long-lasting results and has no after-perm odor or lingering effects. A salon-tested neutralizing agent delivers a fresh clean scent.

LOGICS®
INTERNATIONAL

powerful

IN TODAY'S WORLD, EDUCATION IS POWER. ADULTS EVERYWHERE ARE SEEKING EDUCATION TO REMAIN COMPETITIVE, TO ADVANCE CAREERS, AND FOR PERSONAL SATISFACTION. BUT MANY ADULT LEARNERS HAVE WORK AND FAMILY OBLIGA- TIONS, MAKING IT DIFFICULT TO ATTEND TRADITIONAL CLASS- ES. THEY NEED AN EDUCATION ALTERNATIVE SUCH AS MIND EXTENSION UNIVERSITY* (ME/U) THE EDUCATION NETWORK.™ WITH ME/U, TIME AND DIS- TANCE ARE NO LONGER A PROBLEM. ALL YOU HAVE TO DO IS TURN IT ON!

"ME/U'S PURPOSE IS TO CRE- ATE A GREAT SCHOOL, AN ELECTRONIC CAMPUS FILLED WITH EXCITEMENT THAT MAKE...

accessi

ME/U REACHE... MILLION HOME... AND SCHOOLS T... AND SATELLITE STUDENTS CAN THROUGHOUT NO... CENTRAL AMERICA ... NORTHERN-MOST PA... SOUTH AMERICA. GLOB... ME/U ALSO REACHES WO... WIDE TO LONDON, MUNI... AND BANGKOK. BUSINESS NE... WORKS SUCH AS THE AIRPOR... NEWS AND TRAINING NETWORK, AND PUBLIC ACCESS CHAN- NELS AROUND THE COUNTRY, USE ME/U AS A SOURCE FOR SUPPLEMENTAL CURRICULUM. IN ADDITION, MOST ME/U COURSES ARE AVAILABLE ON VIDEO. TAPES NOT ONLY PRO- VIDE CONVENIENCE FOR STU- DENTS LOCATED IN REMOTE LOCATIONS, THEY ADD FLEXI- BILITY FOR BUSY ADULTS. THROUGH ME/U, STUDENTS CAN ATTEND CLASSES ANY- WHERE, ANYTIME.

education is
knowledge

mind

extension

EDUCATION IS POWER IN TODAYS WORLD.
education
is power
WITH DISTANCE LEARNING PROGRAMS FROM
MIND EXTENSION UNIVERSITY (ME/U) ALL YOU

HAVE TO DO IS TURN IT ON!

university

turn it on

client
mind extension university
design firm
vaughn wedeen creative
art director/designer
steve wedeen
photographers
michael barley   don bonsey

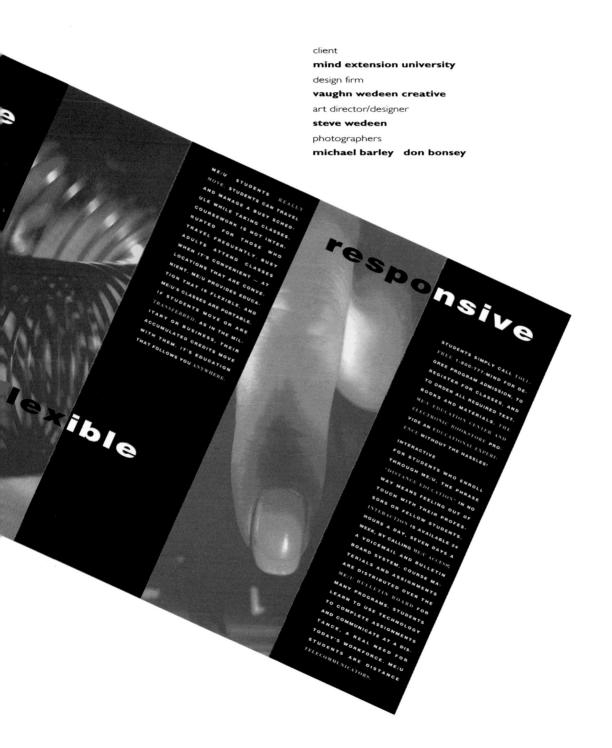

responsive

flexible

ME/U STUDENTS REALLY MOVE. STUDENTS CAN TRAVEL AND MANAGE A BUSY SCHEDULE WHILE TAKING CLASSES. COURSEWORK IS NOT INTERRUPTED FOR THOSE WHO TRAVEL FREQUENTLY. BUSY ADULTS ATTEND CLASSES WHEN IT'S CONVENIENT ... AT LOCATIONS THAT ARE CONVENIENT. ME/U PROVIDES EDUCATION THAT IS FLEXIBLE. AND ME/U'S CLASSES ARE PORTABLE. IF STUDENTS MOVE OR ARE TRANSFERRED, AS IN THE MILITARY OR BUSINESS, THEIR ACCUMULATED CREDITS MOVE WITH THEM. IT'S EDUCATION THAT FOLLOWS YOU ANYWHERE.

STUDENTS SIMPLY CALL TOLL-FREE 1-800-777-MIND FOR DEGREE PROGRAM ADMISSION, TO REGISTER FOR CLASSES, AND TO ORDER ALL REQUIRED TEXTBOOKS AND MATERIALS. THE ME/U EDUCATION CENTER AND ELECTRONIC BOOKSTORE PROVIDE AN EDUCATIONAL EXPERIENCE WITHOUT THE HASSLES!

INTERACTIVE FOR STUDENTS WHO ENROLL THROUGH ME/U, THE PHRASE "DISTANCE EDUCATION" IN NO WAY MEANS FEELING OUT OF TOUCH WITH THEIR PROFESSORS OR FELLOW STUDENTS. INTERACTION IS AVAILABLE 24 HOURS A DAY, SEVEN DAYS A WEEK, BY CALLING ME/U ACCESS, A VOICEMAIL AND BULLETIN BOARD SYSTEM. COURSE MATERIALS AND ASSIGNMENTS ARE DISTRIBUTED OVER THE ME/U BULLETIN BOARD FOR MANY PROGRAMS. STUDENTS LEARN TO USE TECHNOLOGY TO COMPLETE ASSIGNMENTS AND COMMUNICATE AT A DISTANCE. A REAL NEED FOR TODAY'S WORKFORCE. ME/U STUDENTS ARE DISTANCE TELECOMMUNICATORS.

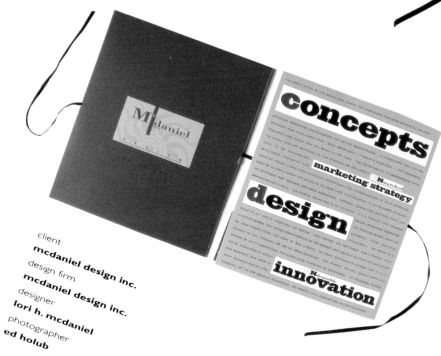

client
mcdaniel design inc.
design firm
mcdaniel design inc.
designer
lori h. mcdaniel
photographer
ed holub

client
s. d. warren
design firm
frankfurt gips balkind
creative director
cheryl heller
designer
ann roquette
photographer
clint clemens

client
metlife capital corporation

design firm
spangler associates inc.

creative director
kathryn spangler

designer
ross hogin

illustrator
kong lu

photographers
m. angelo   louis bencze

مركز المحمل

Al Mahmal Center

client
al mahmal center
design firm
alan chan design company
creative director
alan chan

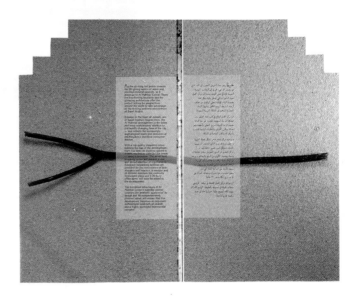

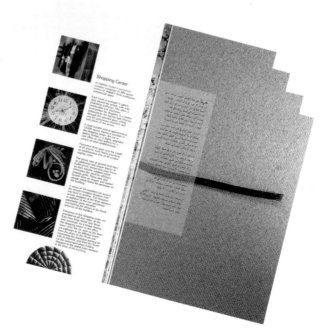

client
greg heck photography
design firm
segura inc.
designer
carlos segura
photographer
greg heck

client
cross pointe paper corporation
design firm
little & company
designer
ted riley
photographers
steve kemmerling
michael northrup

What you see is what you get. **Fat chance.**

With all the changes in design, color and printing technologies, it takes more than a good set of eyes to be sure what you get on press is what you want.

THAT'S WHY proofs are so important. They are your only chance to make sure your job matches your expectations before you get to the printer. Laserscan gives you all kinds of options, including a growing array of electronically prepared proofs. We'll even prepare proofs on different stocks and substrates, so you get the most accurate view of how your project will look when it's completed. Combine that with how we prepare film to match your printer's precise specifications and you know you'll end up with the best job possible.

client
laserscan
design firm
after hours creative
creative director
russ haan
designer
dino paul

U.S. SAVINGS BONDS ★ 1994 CAMPAIGN

VISIONS

OF AMERICA

client
nynex corporation
design firm
belk mignogna associates ltd.
art directors
steve mignogna
wendy blattner
designers
wendy blattner
donna dornbusch

client
herman miller, inc.
design firm
herman miller, inc.
designers
kathy stanton   yang kim
vic hewitt
illustrators
gould design   mick wiggins

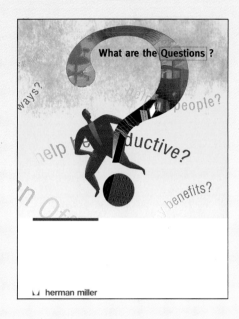

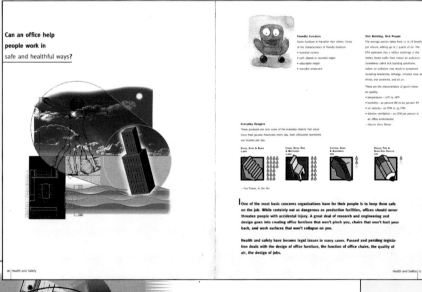

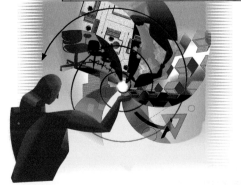

client
nike inc.
design firm
nike design
art director/designer
john norman
photographer
eric pearle

client
new york zoological society,
the wildlife conservation society
design firm
drenttel doyle partners
creative directors
stephen doyle   tom kluepfel
designers
rosemarie turk   mats hakansson
chuck robertson   gary tooth

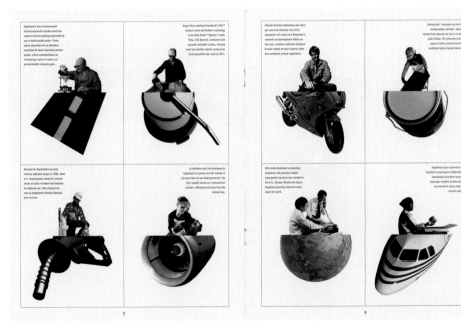

client
engelhard corporation
design firm
cook and shanosky associates inc.
art directors
roger cook   don shanosky
photographers
carol fatta   douglas mellor
peter vidor

NIKE WOMEN'S SPORTS AND FITNESS →IT'S TIME

Strength. NIKE ANSWERS THIS CRY

BODY CONDITIONING. THE PINNACLE

...'S FITNESS. SLIDE TRAINER. HAND WEIGHTS

...R. THE STEP — IT'S A **MULTI-ACTIVITY**

RESISTANCE TRAINING

...OUT BEYOND ANYTHING THAT'S BEEN DONE

...FORE. NOT JUST BUTTS AND GUTS, THIS **WORKOUT**

ENCOMPASSES EVERY MUSCLE GROUP THAT WOMEN

WEIGHT TRAINING

POSSESS. **TOTAL BODY CONDITIONING,** IT'S

THE ULTIMATE **IN-STUDIO**

CONDITIONING

WORKOUT. WHO EVER SAID **WOMEN** ARE THE

SLIDE TRAINING

WEAKER SEX IS IN FOR A SURPRISE.

THE SHOES

TOTAL BODY CONDITIONING SHOES ARE EXCEP-
TIONALLY PREPARED FOR MULTI-EQUIPMENT

STEP TRAINING

INTERACTION PROVIDING THE ULTIMATE IN
FOREFOOT CUSHIONING. LATERAL STABILITY,
DURABILITY AND BREATHABILITY.

AIR TOTAL BODY 2010

When women move THEY'RE NOT DANCIN'

TO SOMEONE ELSE'S BEAT. THEY'RE SETTING THE PACE.

IT'S **FAST** AND IT'S HOT. FULL OF HIP HOP, PUMPIN'

AND JUMPIN'. SOME CALL IT **FUNK.** OR AN IN-STUDIO

INTERPRETATION OF THE **RHYTHM** OF THE STREET.

SIDE 1 DANCE AEROBICS IS A CROSS BETWEEN

MOTION AND EMOTION. WHEN YOU GET DOWN TO

IT, IT'S FITNESS WITH AN **ATTITUDE.** IF YOU

DON'T THINK YOU CAN

KEEP UP, JUST WATCH. BUT LET THE SPECTATOR

BEWARE — IT'LL **MOVE** YOU.

M O V E   I T

D A N C E   I T

W O R K   I T

SIDE 1

THE SHOES

DESIGNED TO PROVIDE THE FLUID TRACTION

NECESSARY FOR HOT, HIP-HOP DANCE CHOREO-

GRAPHY. SIDE 1 SHOES OFFER FUNCTIONAL

PERFORMANCE WITHOUT SACRIFICING FINESSE.

STANCE

client
nike women's division
design firm
nike design
art director/designer
valerie taylor smith
illustrator
gary hush
photographer
cliff watts

client
new oji
design firm
jensen design associates
creative director
david jensen
designer
mark biro

If you think a baby's bottom is smooth, feel this. Few textures can compare to the per-

fectly smooth, unblemished surface of a baby's skin. Softness so desirable, you want to

pick it up. The same is true of TopKote Dull. The exceptionally smooth surface makes

ink coverage sit up and be noticed. The texture of TopKote Dull allows for uniform ink

lay and excellent hold out. Printed materials appear sharp and clear against the

smooth surface of TopKote Dull. Like the feel of a baby, TopKote Dull is good to the touch.

© Julie Gang Photography, NYC 212-925-3351

ROMAN ANTIQUE
GOLD DINNERWARE

Set your table with style.
Roman Antique 24K gold
banded glass tableware is
versatile and extraordinarily
durable. Available in 21
different sizes.

Use these thick rustic glass
pieces as dinnerplates or
to serve chocolate truffles,
fruit, or hors d'oeuvres.

ART COMES TO THE TABLE

ANNIEGLASS

client
annieglass
design firm
russell leong design
designers
russell k. leong
pam m. matsuda
betsy todd
photographer
r. j. muna

Maybe I'll go to Amsterdam, maybe I'll go to Rome, and rent me a grand piano and put some flowers 'round my room.
– JONI MITCHELL

The journey, not the arrival, matters.
– T.S. ELIOT

Welcome to O'H

Now departing from gate 4

estimated time of arrival

On time

Now arri

severe storm warning in effect for Chicago and vicini

...mated time of departure 8:29

client
consolidated papers, inc.

design firm
liska and associates, inc.

art director
steve liska

designer
valerie cote

photographer
tim bieber

6:00 am

over 7,700 acres

There is no other airport in the world

about 175,000 everyday

which serves so many people and

so many airplanes. an average of 110 arrive or depart each hour

This is an extraordinary airport,

"What is the city but the people?" – WILLIAM SHAKESPEARE

an extraordinary city,

the busiest airport in the world

and an extraordinary country, and it (O'Hare)

could be classed as one of the wonders of the modern world.

– JOHN F. KENNEDY, 1963

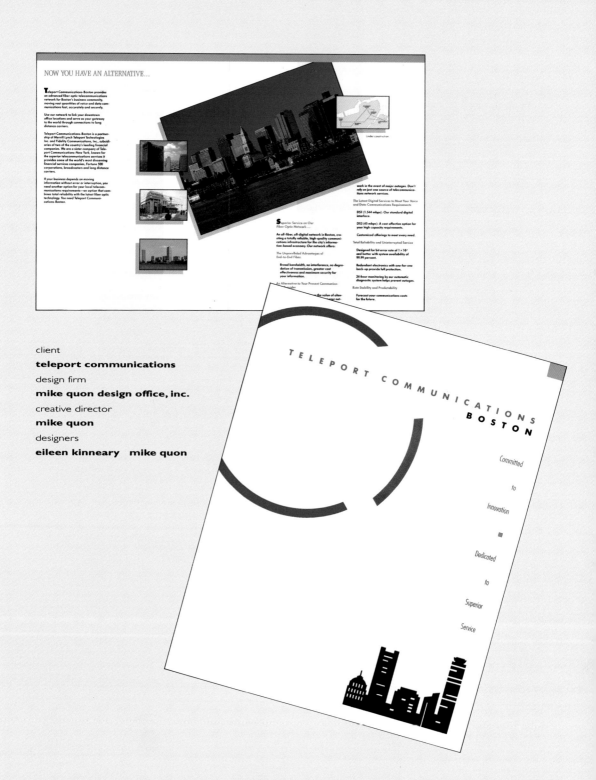

client
teleport communications
design firm
mike quon design office, inc.
creative director
mike quon
designers
eileen kinneary   mike quon

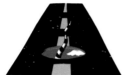

client
potlatch/kvester group

design firm
frazier design

creative director
craig frazier

designers
craig frazier
rené rosso

illustrator
craig frazier

The act of compromising finds the designer right between compliance and his conscience, with all eyes on him.

The idea of it isn't really that awful, it's more the worry that you are going out the door of originality right into the mouth of mediocrity.

client
international paper
design firm
oden & associates
art director
bret terwilleger
illustrators
david meyer   jill broadhacker
guy stieferman   bill berry
photographer
chip pankey

client
insurance conference planners
association (icpa)
design firm
sayles graphic design
art director/designer
john sayles
illustrator
john sayles

reports

client
the black & decker corporation
design firm
cook and shanosky associates inc.
art directors
roger cook   don shanosky
designers
roger cook   don shanosky
douglas baszczuk
photographer
tom francisco

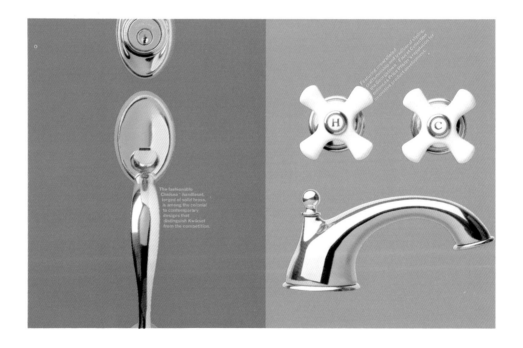

client
snap-on inc.
design firm
thiel visual design
designers
john thiel   jim pitroski
photographer
john nienhuis

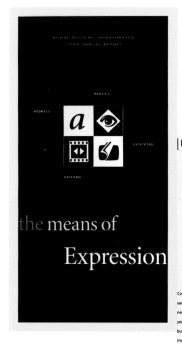

client
adobe systems inc.
design firm
frankfurt balkind partners
creative directors
kent hunter   aubrey balkind
designer
kin yeun
illustrator
henrik drescher
photographers
jeffrey newbury   jock mcdonald
julie powell

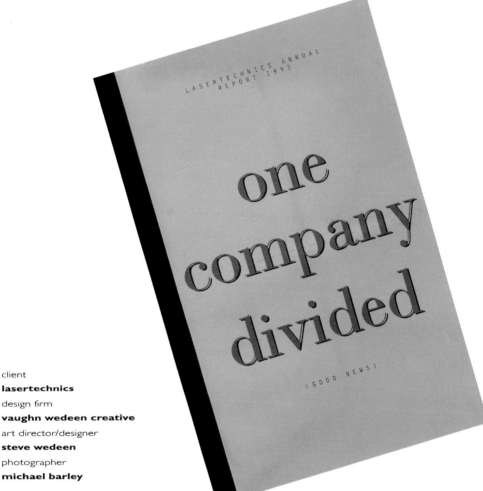

client
lasertechnics
design firm
vaughn wedeen creative
art director/designer
steve wedeen
photographer
michael barley

client
montefiore medical center
design firm
mike quon design office, inc.
art directors
diane bennett   mike quon
designers
jan wohlenberg   erick kuo
steve newman
illustrator
mike quon
photographer
lisa seifert

PAST is Present

Remember when? When your family's doctor was available to you around the clock? When you didn't have to sift through your aches and pains to decide

Welcome back. If a family doctor is and thought you would never have Montefiore Medical Group's River and rediscover the one-to-one do you've been missing.

PRESENT

eties

PRESENT

P R E S E N T

MONTEFIORE MEDICAL GROUP
FAMILY PRACTICE OFFICE IN RIVERDALE

PAST

Present

718-884-4201

5626

FAMILY Practice
in the NINETIES

You may be old enough to remember the doctor coming to your house with his little black bag. Those days, for the most part, are over. But the days of the GP have been revitalized—through family practice. We're trained in all branches of medicine and in the intricate workings of family life, too. Primary care doctors provide patient and family with a stable, continuing, physician's presence.

We believe that total care for an individual involves more than medical care for problems. We know that family practice is at the forefront of preventive care, and we coordinate all facets of that care (eye, podiatry, home health care, surgery–both major and minor–and hospitalization). As we care for the individual's illness, we develop an insight into the ongoing stresses and the medical problems of the whole family.

want

o the

ractice,

ationship

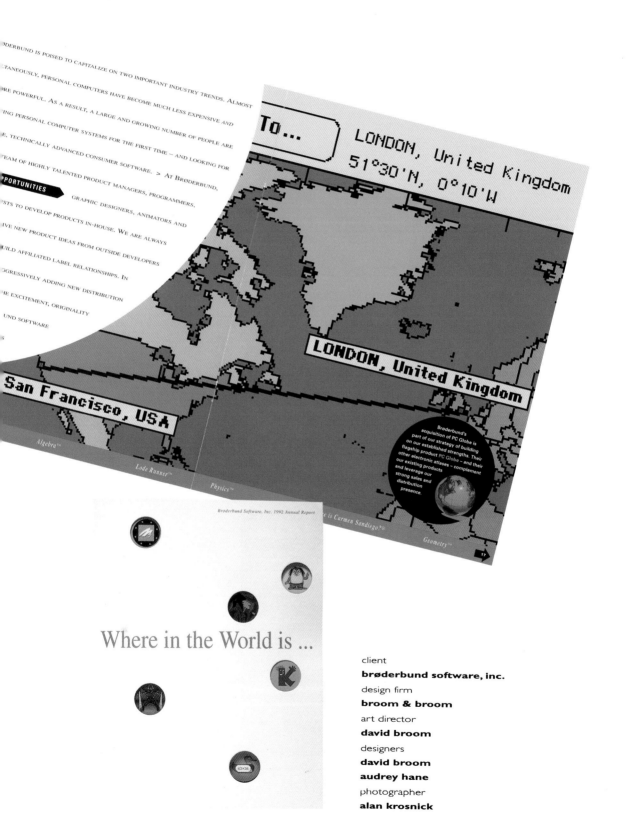

ⁿDERBUND IS POISED TO CAPITALIZE ON TWO IMPORTANT INDUSTRY TRENDS. ALMOST

-TANEOUSLY, PERSONAL COMPUTERS HAVE BECOME MUCH LESS EXPENSIVE AND

ⁿRE POWERFUL. AS A RESULT, A LARGE AND GROWING NUMBER OF PEOPLE ARE

ⁿING PERSONAL COMPUTER SYSTEMS FOR THE FIRST TIME – AND LOOKING FOR

ⁿE, TECHNICALLY ADVANCED CONSUMER SOFTWARE. > AT BRØDERBUND,

ⁿEAM OF HIGHLY TALENTED PRODUCT MANAGERS, PROGRAMMERS,

PORTUNITIES   GRAPHIC DESIGNERS, ANIMATORS AND

ⁿSTS TO DEVELOP PRODUCTS IN-HOUSE. WE ARE ALWAYS

ⁿVE NEW PRODUCT IDEAS FROM OUTSIDE DEVELOPERS

ⁿUILD AFFILIATED LABEL RELATIONSHIPS. IN

ⁿGGRESSIVELY ADDING NEW DISTRIBUTION

ⁿE EXCITEMENT, ORIGINALITY

ⁿUND SOFTWARE

To...   LONDON, United Kingdom
51°30'N, 0°10'W

LONDON, United Kingdom

San Francisco, USA

Algebra™

Lode Runner™

Physics™

Brøderbund Software, Inc. 1992 Annual Report   ...e is Carmen Sandiego?®

Geometry™

17

Brøderbund's acquisition of PC Globe is part of our strategy of building on our established strengths. Their flagship product PC Globe – and their other electronic atlases – complement our existing products and leverage our strong sales and distribution presence.

Where in the World is ...

client
brøderbund software, inc.
design firm
broom & broom
art director
david broom
designers
david broom
audrey hane
photographer
alan krosnick

client
rasterops corporation
design firm
howry design associates
creative director
jill howry
designer
julie lantz taylor
photographers
**bob & lois schlowsky,
schlowsky photography**

RasterOps 1993 Annual Report

Keeping the Competitive Edge

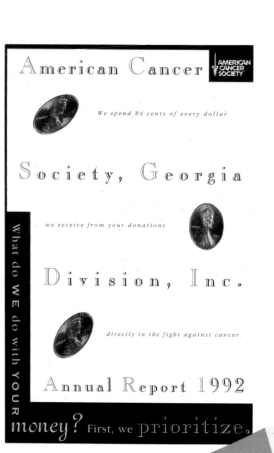

client
**american cancer society,
georgia division inc.**
design firm
corporate reports inc.
art director/designer
brant day
illustrator
brant day
photographer
jerry burns

COMSAT ON COURSE: A ROUNDTABLE DISCUSSION

Atlantic. We moved very quickly to procure a satellite that has become known as the INTELSAT-K. It is online right now and offers very high power to very small dishes. We also continuously plan new services. For example, we're working on "bandwidth-on-demand," a service that will enable private line customers to pay only for the capacity they use.

DRAMATIC UPSWINGS IN PUBLIC SWITCHED TELEPHONY—INCREASES of 20% TO 40% ANNUALLY—HAVE COME OUTSIDE THE WORLD'S MATURE ECONOMIES.

ANNUAL GROWTH IN INTERNATIONAL PUBLIC SWITCHED TELEPHONE NETWORKS
- Mature markets
- Immature markets/developed countries
- Developing countries
by percent

On COMSAT's Outlook: Crockett: We will tend to look outside the U.S. for our markets and to vertically integrate towards international customers. That's an overt strategy because we see fallow ground almost everywhere we look around the world. Fifty-five percent of the world's population does not have dial tone. We have ways to give them that service. Mario: There's a very real connection between COMSAT's businesses. The strategy Charlie is following in On Command Video is very much a follow-on to what we have been doing in mobile communications. There are different platforms, but what we're doing is segmenting the market and then providing value-added services.

On Staying the Course: Crockett: It turns out that changing a company's culture is a whole lot harder than they tell you about in business school. As I said in last year's report, you just don't go out and kiss babies and make speeches, and the culture changes. So, we're going through a radical cultural change, a reorientation of a company that has been focused on technology and engineering to one that has bias for customer service, and it is a process that isn't over yet. Alewine: Not too long ago, when a customer came to us, COMSAT would tell them what we thought they needed. And it was almost always over-engineered and cost too much. Now, we listen very carefully to what customers tell us about *their* needs. Crockett: If you spend half your life worrying about customers, and the other half worrying about the competition, you'll probably end up doing very well.

18

CHRISTINE A. KING ■ MANAGER, SYSTEMS ANALYSIS SOFTWARE ■ COMSAT LABORATORIES

HOW MUCH TRAFFIC CAN A SATELLITE HANDLE IN A THUNDERSTORM? CALL CHRIS KING'S 20-PERSON-STRONG TEAM OF SATELLITE-MAXIMIZING ANALYSIS FOR THE ANSWER. THE SYSTEMS ANALYSIS SOFTWARE GROUP AT COMSAT LABORATORIES, WITH ITERATION OF STRIP (SATELLITE TRANSMISSION IMPAIRMENTS PROGRAM), WHICH HAS ENABLED SERVICE WITH 99.99 PERCENT RELIABILITY.

COMSAT ON COURSE

client
comsat corporation
design firm
the graphic expression, inc.
creative director
steve ferrari
photographers
eric myer   george bennett

People expect to go anywhere and still communicate. ■ You can't tie a fiber optic cable to the end of an airplane or a ship or a human being. ■ What we've done is sharpen the focus of COMSAT on the niches which match our capabilities. ■ If you spend half your life worrying about customers, and the other half worrying about the competition, you'll probably end up doing very well. ■ When we look back on what shaped this era, we'll say the single biggest force was the ability to communicate at will around the world.

client
marcam corporation
design firm
polese clancy
creative director
ellen clancy
designer
tom riddle
illustrator
jeff koegel
photographer
george simian

client
metropolitan life

design firm
belk mignogna associates ltd.

art director
howard belk

designers
wendy blattner   victor russo

illustrators
peter lo bianco
united feature syndicate inc.

photographers
peter greoire   karl nemecek
barry rosenthal

Mead:
working smarter, faster, better.

Mead

client
the mead corporation

design firm
addison corporate annual reports

art director/designer
john march

illustrator
eliot bergman

Our capacity for positive solutions has never been greater.

Mead employees have become more and more focused on results than at any time in our history. We've come to expect more from ourselves. We're challenging old ways of working, and rethinking how we manage our businesses. Teamwork remains essential, but every team is only as strong as each individual's performance. At Mead, each person is accountable for delivering results, setting and meeting high expectations and transforming Mead into a high performing organization.

Mead's High Performance Management Index

We've raised the bar on performance at Mead. In 1991, our top 500 managers rated themselves average. Yet one vision clearly called for world class performers. So we put a stake in the ground and set our sights on measured improvement. We examined how we worked, what we did, why we did it. Today a successful Mead manager is results-oriented, committed to change and focused on customers and shared values. We've got a way to go, but progress to date shows we think we're way above average and on the way to world class.

client
the black & decker corporation
design firm
cook and shanosky associates inc.
art directors
roger cook   don shanosky
designers
roger cook   don shanosky
cathryn cook
photographer
tom francisco

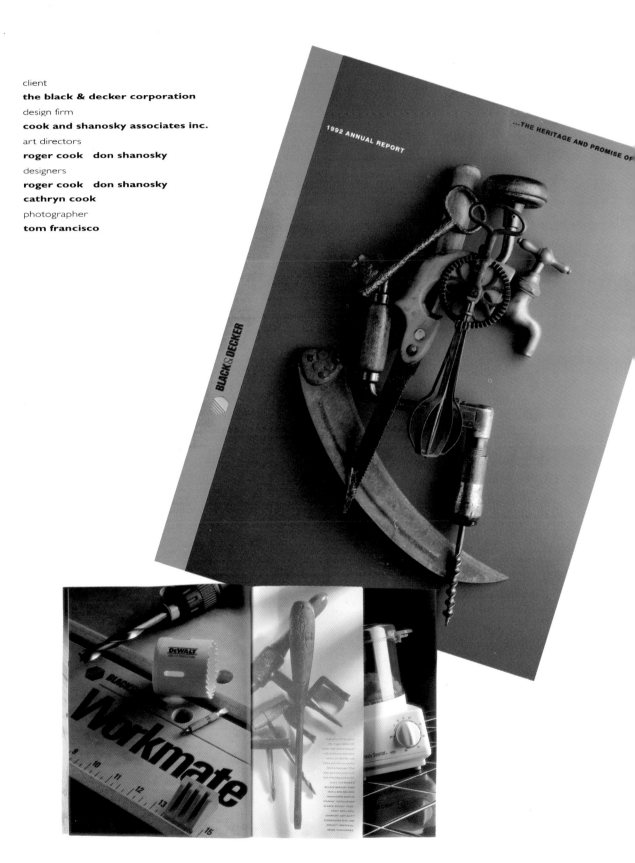

client
omi corp.
design firm
the graphic expression, inc.
creative director
steve ferrari
designer
steven flamm
photographers
vickers & beechler
steve firebaugh

client
the neiman marcus group, inc.
design firm
belk mignogna associates ltd.
art director
steve mignogna
designers
victoria stamm   jennifer choi
photographers
richard dunkley
jose picayo

client
nike inc.
design firm
nike design
art director/designer
ann schwiebinger
illustrator
joel nakamura
photographers
**amy guip   james wojcik
jose picayo   gary hush
charles purvis   maria robledo
grace knott   geof kern**

client
expeditors international
design firm
leimer cross design
creative director/art director
kerry leimer
designer
craig terrones
illustrator
bonnie scranton
photographers
tyler boley   jeff corwin

out with the old, in with the profitable

[We have sold or dropped products with diminishing returns in favor of proven products with ongoing potential.]

Lasertechnics to (1) expand globally, (2) build partnerships to provide total system solutions, (3) diversify product applications, (4) maintain and enhance our technological lead, and (5) boost operating efficiency. Working within the strategic plan, we have reorganized our priorities and refocused our resources. For example, we have placed a much stronger emphasis on customer service. We recently opened a new East Coast office that serves as a base for both our regional sales manager and a service technician. This tactic brings Lasertechnics service closer to our customers and enables us to respond more quickly. The sales manager and service technician work together to close orders, which should expand our service contract business. Our customers are responding very positively.

Our new priorities also affect Lasertechnics' Imaging Division. The DIR Gray Scale Printer has been the workhorse of this division. Its strengths are its speed, high resolution and low media cost; the one weakness it has faced is connectivity, which is a problem not with the printer but with the software drivers that interface it to host personal computers. We are working to overcome this problem.

Lasertechnics Annual Report 1992

back to basics

[a dramatic new direction]

client
lasertechnics, inc.
design firm
vaughn wedeen creative
art director/designer
steve wedeen

client
phoenix re corporation
design firm
thomas ryan design
photographer
jeff frazier photography

client
**san francisco
airport commission**
design firm
morla design
art director
jennifer morla
designers
**jennifer morla
craig bailey**
photographer
holly stewart

client
**kansas elks training
center for the handicapped**
design firm
gardner + greteman
art directors
**bill gardner
sonia greteman**
designer
james strange
illustrators
**bill gardner
james strange**

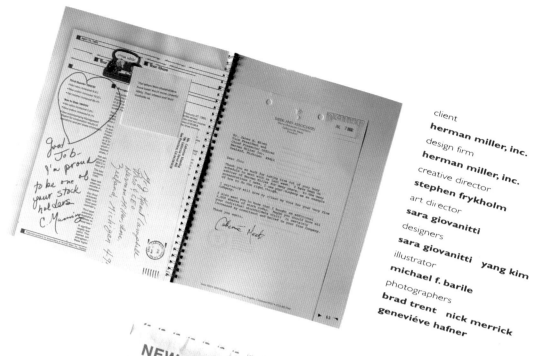

client
herman miller, inc.
design firm
herman miller, inc.
creative director
stephen frykholm
art director
sara giovanitti
designers
sara giovanitti   yang kim
illustrator
michael f. barile
photographers
**brad trent   nick merrick
geneviéve hafner**

client
advo inc.
design firm
zahor & bender inc.
art directors
d. bruce zahor   roy bender
designer
christina mausser
illustrators
rosemary webber   paul zinolak
gary baseman   adam cohen
rob coglin
photographer
john earle

Own
the top name
brand in the
category

Possess
a very strong
market share

Capitalize
on global
markets

1993 financial
report

Tambrands

ANNUAL REPORT | 1993

client
tambrands inc.

design firm
belk mignogna associates ltd.

art directors
howard belk   steve mignogna

designers
lisa klausing   donna dornbusch

photographers
barry rosenthal   peter marlowe
stephen begleighter   jon love

United Water Resources **1993 ANNUAL REPORT**

client
united water resources
design firm
the graphic expression, inc.
creative director
steve ferrari
designer
sue balle
illustrators
liz wheaton
mike kowalski
photographers
bob day
kelly/mooney

With the acquisition of two refineries during 1993, Tosco has become the second largest independent oil refiner in the United States, as measured by throughput. ✦ Tosco's three refineries — the Avon refinery, operated by Tosco Refining Company; the Bayway refinery, operated by Bayway Refining Company; and the Ferndale refinery, operated by Tosco Northwest Company — process more than 500,000 barrels per day of crude oil and other feedstocks. ✦ Input and transportation fuel production volumes at the three refineries in 1993 are as follows:

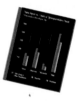

client
tosco corporation
design firm
the graphic expression, inc.
creative director
steve ferrari
designer
kurt finkbeiner
photographers
rod del pozo   brian peterson

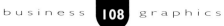
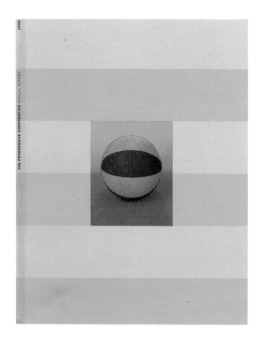

client
the progressive corporation
design firm
nesnadny & schwartz
creative directors
mark schwartz   **joyce nesnadny**
designers
joyce nesnadny   **michelle moehler**
photographer
neil winokur

client
the promus companies

design firm
the graphic expression, inc.

creative director
steve ferrari

designer
steven flamm

photographer
jim barber

The Promus Companies • 1993 Annual Report • Book One

THE TOP
Reasons
Why
10
PROMUS
is an OUTSTANDING
Company
1993 Annual Report

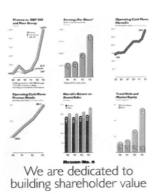

We are dedicated to
building shareholder value

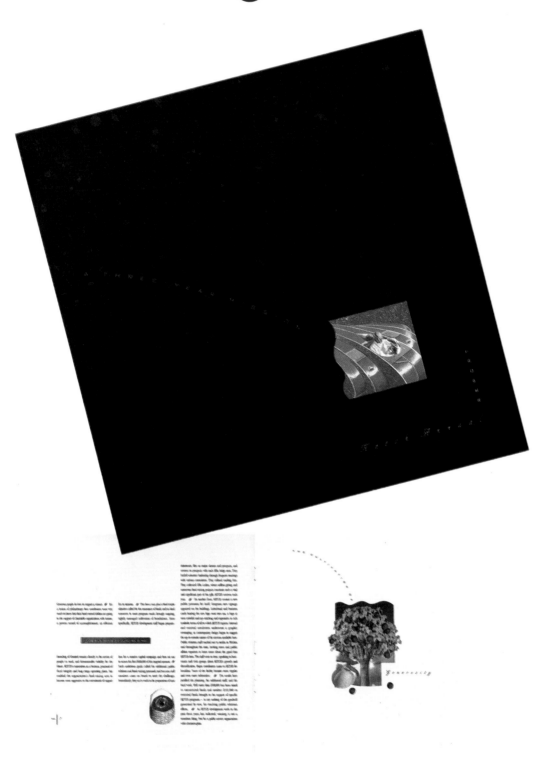

client
**kansas elks training center
for the handicapped**
design firm
gardner + greteman
art directors
bill gardner   sonia greteman
designer
james strange
illustrators
bill gardner   james strange

client
georgia-pacific corporation
design firm
samata associates
art directors
jim hardy   greg samata
designer
jim hardy
photographers
marc norberg   sandro miller

©1994 Georgia-Pacific Corporation

Georgia-Pacific
A n n u a l
Report
1 9 9 3

During 1993, Marshall Hahn retired as Georgia-Pacific's chairman and chief executive officer. Under his leadership, the company accelerated its assets, sales and cash flow and emerged as one of the world's leading forest products companies. More important, Marshall instilled a culture of value creation that will continue to serve G-P's shareholders for years to come.

Building Products
grow on nearly
six million acres of
timberland owned
by Georgia-Pacific. It is
a farm like no other:
A rotating, renewable
resource that annually yields
lumber, plywood, oriented strand board,
residual chips for pulp and paper, and provides
all the other benefits of a working forest.
The forest is an essential part of our long-standing
position as one of America's leading manufacturers
and distributors of building products. It provides the foundation
for a system of manufacturing and distribution
that is unrivaled in our industry.

client
knowledgeware
design firm
corporate reports inc.
art director/designer
brant day
illustrators
**brant day   vivienne flesher
joan hersey   thom sevalrud
joel nakamura**
photographer
jonathan hillyer

KnowledgeWare®

Vision
in
Action

Annual Report
1 9 9 3

Distribu
A NEW GLOBAL

The Headlines of the Year 1993

a big welcome for ADW 2.7

The introduction of ADW® 2.7 — one of the most significant events ever in the application development industry — signaled the completion of the largest development project in KnowledgeWare's history. It was only fitting that its rollout should also set new industry standards for quality. Method: From January through March, free seminars in 17 cities were conducted by product managers and developers to provide customers with the information needed to take full advantage of the new release.

Legacy Workbench
Unveiled at International User Conference

For more than three decades, many companies have invested serious amounts of time and money into the development of COBOL applications. They are just as serious about protecting those investments. Legacy Workbench,™ the cornerstone of the industry's most comprehensive redevelopment solution, is a powerful suite of tools that assess, document, restructure, and graphically maintain those existing systems. Considering that the average IS department spends up to 80 percent of its budget on maintaining mainframe-based systems, the marketing opportunities for the Legacy Workbench are significant.

During fiscal year 1993, inter total revenues. According over the approaching ye cial benefits — of that International the Fi KnowledgeWare V offices in 12 cou

N
Par
To
Nor

ForeSight Replaces Development Guesswork

More than ever, due to the intensified complexity of client/server technology, effective and efficient development depends on having a clear, precise blueprint to follow from the beginning. ForeSight,™ which came to KnowledgeWare through the acquisition of Computer and Engineering Consultants, is built within the ADW encyclopedia and offers a dynamic and automated methodology for ADW customers. Due to its adaptability, ForeSight is already enhancing the use — and accelerating the benefits — of our products at customer sites such as Ford, Whirlpool, and Wisconsin Power and Light.

Flash-point
Making the Old New

Flashpoint® (acquired during fiscal 1993) came to market this year under the KnowledgeWare banner. Its key selling point could not be more timely. Flashpoint brings legacy mainframe applications into the world of client/server by creating graphical interfaces and integrating old and new applications at the user's desktop.

Revenues for Professional Services Grow 100 Perce

As the complexity of technology has continued to increase, so demand for training and consulting. To keep pace with ma KnowledgeWare acquired Computer and Engineering Co organization that specialized in providing consulting se customers, to form the foundation of a new Professio sion. The impact was immediate. A 100% in rev

ObjectView: Building for the Future

As the popularity of moving to client/server rose during fiscal 1993, so did the clamor for tools to build new client/server applications. In February 1993, we acquired ObjectView,™ a powerful tool for rapid development of new client/server
seriously undervalued and undermarketed, the prod-
the war for client/server market share.

Vision in Action

The power to anticipate the reality that lies ahead makes a company visionary. The Readiness to act on that reality makes a company a leader. It is more than the difference between seeing and doing. It is the difference between offering fixed solutions for changing needs and the agility to answer change with change. It is this difference that defines KnowledgeWare's front-line strategy and assures its leadership position.

A 4th Quarter for the Record Books ! ! !

The sweeping changes at KnowledgeWare were not undertaken lightly. Nor were they carried out without a sense of confidence, for we were sure they represented the most direct route to our goals. Revenues for the fourth quarter of fiscal 1993 were $40,426,000, compared to $34,493,000 in the same period last year. Net income for the quarter totalled $2,779,000 or $0.21 per share, compared to fiscal 1992 fourth quarter net profit of $2,336,000 or $0.18 per share.

Y

…d 27.9 percent of …entage will expand …nd increase the finan- …ired from Ernst & Young …rt our products in Europe. … Paris and includes 16 branch

Investment Cost

KnowledgeWare's accomplishments in 1993 were made possible by investments throughout the fiscal year. The Matesys acquisition, the establishment of international operations, the release of ADW 2.7, and the staffing of Professional Services all had significant associated costs. As a result, the company reported a net loss for the year of $25,799,000, or $1.94 per share. However, our record-setting fourth quarter shows early results. Undoubtedly, these investments will position us for growth in years ahead.

…ne's Benefit

…d rely on single vendors for most hardware and …nore. In today's open, non-proprietary world, an …n could easily involve components from at least 25 …dgeWare has always been committed to open systems …ntinue to work with a long list of companies important to … new names on the list this year include Hewlett-Packard, … Digital, Intel, Oracle, Sybase, and Microsoft.

Continued Overall Growth

According to *Software Magazine*, July 1993, KnowledgeWare was ranked the 31st largest software company in the world, up from 36th largest in 1992. Revenues for 1993 were at $128,761,000, compared with $116,542,000 in 1992. And our installed base, the primary indicator of our market influence, was at 118,000 units at the end of fiscal 1993.

…fing for New …portunities

…completion of ADW 2.7 and the addition of new products, expanded …s, and international operations, KnowledgeWare's organization had to …ge. We restructured our work force to align it with business objectives and …allocated headcount to growth areas such as client/server, consulting, and …nternational operations.

America Online 1993 Annual Report

client
america online inc.

design firm
broom & broom

art director
david broom

designers
david broom
deborah hagemann

illustrator
gene greif

photographer
steve sherman

a new, interactive, medium is emerging, and it will change the way we inform, educate, work and play

Welcome to America Online

client
comsat corporation
design firm
the graphic expression, inc.
creative director
steve ferrari
designer
kurt finkbeiner
illustrator
mick wiggins
photography
bob day
stock photography

Like The Blossoming

Of A Beautiful Flower,

Horizon Healthcare

Continues To Expand,

Offering New Services

To Meet The Healthcare

Needs Of Our Patients

And Their Families.

Annual Report 1993

client
horizon healthcare corporation
design firm
vaughn wedeen creative
art directors
rick vaughn   daniel michael flynn
designer
daniel michael flynn
photographer
valerie santagto

client
duracell international, inc.
design firm
frankfurt balkind partners
creative directors
aubrey balkind   kent hunter
designer
ruth diener
photographer
michael llewellyn

Superior Products + **Consumer Value Added** + **Effective Advertising** + **Strong Trade Alliances**

client
king world productions
design firm
addison corporate
annual reports
designers
victor rivera   dan koh

5:00 PM Review story possibilities for next day's show.

5

The Oprah Winfrey Show is the most successful talk show in television history. An important part of its appeal for both advertisers and stations is the fact that it is the number one daily program among all women demographics, a statistic that is largely responsible for its ranking as the third highest rated strip in syndication for 27 consecutive sweep periods. Another factor is its positive effect as a lead-in on the size of local news audiences. According to Michael Gartner, former President of NBC News, "A lot of people watch your news show because they watch Oprah Winfrey."

client
western water company
design firm
white design
art director
john white
designer
susan garland foti
photography
stock photography

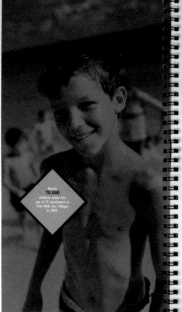

AMERICAN ZONE

What role does the Reservation Center play in Club Med's marketing efforts?

Apart from actual village stays, GMs and their travel agents in the United States have their most important encounter with Club Med through 1-800-CLUB MED, their connection to the Club's Reservation Center in Scottsdale, Arizona. From first inquiry to final confirmation, each encounter must be fast, friendly, and professional. Club Med reservation agents, backed by upgraded software and a sophisticated telephone system that minimize waiting time, are the voice of Club Med to millions of callers annually. Thanks to these enhancements, Scottsdale's average cost per booking has decreased 17.7 percent since 1991. In 1993, increased use of agents for outbound telemarketing, to alert prospective GMs to special promotions and pricing and to promote villages with available capacity, doubled the Club's rate of conversion from reservations options to paid bookings.

Eight American zone villages and three Asian zone villages feature circus workshops, where adults and children can chalk their hands and try their skill on the trapeze. Rollerblading is an increasingly popular alternative exercise at many villages.

How does the company market its product elsewhere in North America?

Club Med's operations in the Canadian market parallel those in the United States, but with differences in demand and in character. The strongest markets are Quebec and metropolitan Toronto and Vancouver. Similar to the approach used in the United States, a dedicated Canadian sales team emphasizes service to the 6 percent of travel agents who account for 53 percent of Canadian bookings. Post-NAFTA Mexico is a clear market of opportunity. As the affluence of Mexican consumers climbs, an increased number of Mexican GMs are expected at the Club's destinations in the Caribbean. In Mexico, our product is marketed from our direct sales office in Mexico City.

Nearly **70,000** children under the age of 12 vacationed at Club Med, Inc. villages in 1993.

AMERICAN ZONE

client
club med, inc.

design firm
the graphic expression, inc.

creative director
steve ferrari

designer
sue balle

illustrator
judy reed

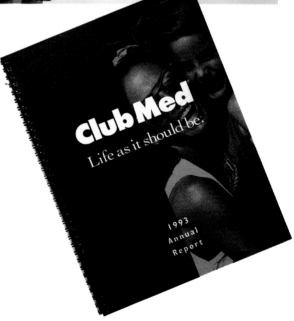

client
reebok international ltd.
design firm
addison corporate
annual reports
art director/designer
victor rivera
photographer
pizzavello

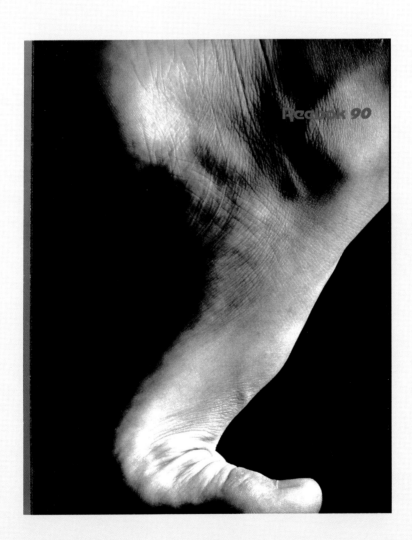

client
us west foundation
design firm
vaughn wedeen creative
art director
steve wedeen
designers
steve wedeen   lisa graff

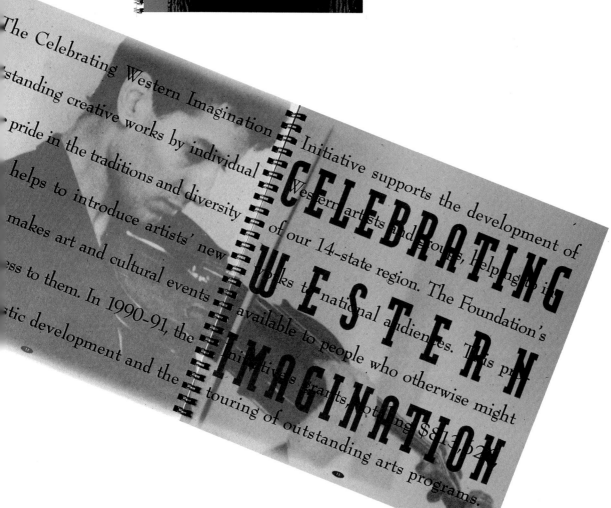

client
presbyterian healthcare
design firm
vaughn wedeen creative
art director/designer
steve wedeen
photographer
valerie santagto

which includes Warner Bros., HBO, and Time Warner Cable. It is capitalized at an agreed-upon value of $20 billion. Our limited partners will invest a total of $1 billion, giving them a 12.5 percent interest in the equity. We expect additional partners to be brought into the alliance. ❯ A sub-venture, Time Warner Entertainment Japan (TWE Japan), which will be owned 50 percent by Time Warner and 25 percent each by Toshiba and C. Itoh, will distribute our home video, theatrical film, television and merchandising products in Japan. TWE Japan will significantly expand our existing businesses in Japan and help develop new opportunities, such as the operation and programming of cable television systems, which Time Warner would not have been able to pursue on its

TIME WARNER ANNOUNCES THE LARGEST-EVER U.S. RIGHTS OFFERING. REVISED AND COMPLETED IN AUGUST. IT IS OVERSUBSCRIBED, RAISING $2.6 BILLION AND REDUCING OUTSTANDING BANK DEBT BY 23 PERCENT.

ATLANTIC'S SKID ROW ENTERS THE BILLBOARD CHARTS AT NR1. THE FOLLOW-ING WEEK, WARNER BROS.' VAN HALEN FOLLOWS IN THE TOP SPOT.

TIME INC. RECONFIGURES ITS A SALES FORCE TO OFFER ADVERT ERS TIME WARNER'S FULL AR OF PRODUCTS AND SERVICES OF FOUR REGIONAL OFF

HBO BEAT THE NETWORKS IN HBO HOMES ON SATURDAY NIGHTS FOR THE 1990-91 SEASON, NIELSEN RATINGS REVEAL—A CABLE INDUSTRY FIRST

Boris Yeltsin in Red Square / Life, "The Year in Pictures"

❯ Our strategic alliance brings to Time Warner partners with an intrinsic understa culture and business environment, and gives us enhanced access to Japanese cons that annual revenues from our TWE businesses in Japan will grow substantially. company, with a growing international presence in the fields of information an also strengthens our global reach. The link with Toshiba means that Time Warn of new media and delivery systems being developed or soon to be on the ma will benefit from the potent programming and distribution resources of **Balance Sheet** Our rights offering last summer enhanced our

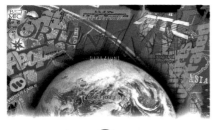

1991 ANNUAL REPORT ● TIMEWARNER

client
time warner, inc.
design firm
frankfurt balkind partners
creative directors
aubrey balkind   kent hunter
designers
ruth diener   kent hunter
illustrators
josh gosfrield   j. d. king
photographer
daon borris

by reducing our debt and demonstrating to potential partners that any alliance would be formed solely on the basis of long-term strategic goals. The offering was oversubscribed and allowed us to pay down approximately $2.6 billion in bank debt — an important step in further securing our financial foundation. In April of 1992, we concluded a $1.1 billion long-term senior debt financing which lengthens the maturity of our debt and helps achieve a better balanced capital structure with less reliance on short-term and medium-term bank debt.

> In addition, Time Warner has investments of its own that performed extremely well in 1991 and brought added value to your company. For example, we own 22 percent of Turner Broadcasting and 14 percent of Hasbro, both

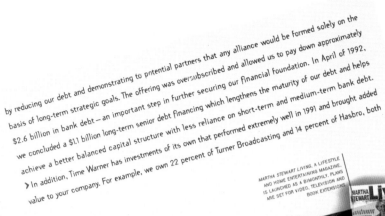

MARTHA STEWART LIVING, A LIFESTYLE AND HOME ENTERTAINING MAGAZINE, IS LAUNCHED AS A BIMONTHLY. PLANS ARE SET FOR VIDEO, TELEVISION AND BOOK EXTENSIONS.

The end of South African apartheid/Time

July

COURT

ROBIN HOOD: PRINCE OF THIEVES IS RELEASED. THE FILM, STARRING KEVIN COSTNER, IS 1991'S NUMBER TWO U.S. BOX OFFICE HIT.

LAUNCH OF COURT TV, BASIC CABLE CHANNEL MANAGED BY TIME WARNER'S AMERICAN LAWYER MEDIA. HEADLINE-MAKING 1991 HIGHLIGHTS INCLUDE CLARENCE THOMAS SENATE CONFIRMA-TION HEARINGS AND THE WILLIAM KENNEDY SMITH RAPE TRIAL.

of whose market values increased substantially in 1991. In fact, by year end, these two investments alone represented $1.6 billion of market value, or the equivalent of approximately $17 per Time Warner common share.

A Year of Performance The underlying strength of Time Warner will always be in our individual businesses. They made 1991 a year of performance and achievement. For 1991 earnings before interest, taxes, depreciation and amortization (EBITDA or operating results, one way that Wall Street often measures cash flow) were $2.26 billion on revenues of $12.02 billion. For the year, we reported a reduced net loss of $99 down from $227 million for 1990. The loss per common share for 1991 was $9.60 after preferred dividends ... of $13.67 per share for 1990. These results for both 1991 and 1990 include noncash

e values, we expect ...ing trading ...ions, C. Itoh the potential ...rtners, in turn, **...tronger** ...strategic alliance

‹ In 1991 Warner Bros.'
feature film division
finished in first place
in domestic box office
share, the fifth time
since 1981, more than
any other studio.

Filmed Entertainment

The Filmed Entertainment division
of Time Warner
is the world's leading producer
and distributor
of theatrical motion pictures,
television programs
and
home videocassette programming.
Warner Bros.'
multifaceted strengths —
management continuity,
creative resources,
marketing skills
and 100 percent-owned
worldwide distribution —
have produced
a record of consistent success
unequalled in the industry.

FINANCIAL HIGHLIGHTS		
(in millions)	1991	1990
Revenues	$3,065	$2,904
EBITDA	$ 390	$ 377

client
the bisys group, inc.

design firm
johnson & simpson
graphic designers

art director
don johnson

designer
bonnie berish

photographers
pierre-yves goavec
dennis connors

BISYS Investment Services Division was established in 1993 with the acquisition of The Barclay Group, Inc. **Investment Services** Barclay provides recordkeeping and administrative services to more than 2,000 corporate-sponsored 401(k) plans throughout the United States.

Barclay's strong management team, history of growth, and recurring revenues met our strategic acquisition criteria, and again extended our single source operating philosophy by providing additional products capable of enhancing the profitability of our client banks.

BISYS targeted the retail industry based on asset growth in 401(k) plans of approximately 30% during the past six years. Industry experts also expect dramatic growth in defined contribution plans offered by companies with 100 to 500 employees, which is Barclay's target market.

During the past decade, Barclay became an industry leader by developing market alliance partnerships with brokerage, insurance, and mutual fund businesses which have national distribution networks to support the sale of their investment products in 401(k) packages. Based on the unique needs of each sponsoring company, Barclay provides a "turnkey" approach to 401(k) administration including state-of-the-art recordkeeping services and daily valuations, participant "800" services, complete loan processing, and customized participant statements.

Significant growth opportunities are provided by existing partners selling additional plans and the development of new partnerships. Potential new business partners include investment managers as well as other entities such as benefits consulting firms, banks currently active in this market segment, and now BISYS' banking clients.

Barclay's hallmark of high client satisfaction, fully featured products and services, and experienced management make the company an excellent complement to BISYS' business units. As one of BISYS' strategic divisions, Barclay gains a strong technology partner focused on increasing service capabilities and both parties gain from the new distribution opportunities with existing client banks.

"The success of any 401 (k) program depends on both investments and recordkeeping. Shearson's area of expertise is investments and we are very sensitive to the recordkeeping aspect of the 401(k) sale. We chose Barclay as our 401 (k) 'strategic alliance partner' because of their responsiveness, proven recordkeeping system and high level of accuracy. Barclay is a valuable partner in our marketing and servicing efforts."

JEFF MILLER
Retirement Plan
Services
Smith Barney
Shearson

fibers

Our accelerated strategy of global growth has the goal of increasing revenues to $9 billion by 1996.

fabric with "Sontara"
protects

jacket of "Nomex"
flame resistant

fashion with "Lycra"
comfort

envelope with "Tyvek"
tear resistant

glove with "Kevlar"
cut resistant

"Stainmaster" carpet
soil resistant

FEDEX PAK

Textiles	"Lycra" spand "Dacron" pol Nylon, "bac
Flooring Systems	"Sontara" fabric, spunbond "Typar" polypre
Nonwovens	
Industrial Nylon	Nylon
Advanced Materials	"Kev ara

Fibers had 1992 sales of $6.1 billion, representing 16.1 perc
with the goal of increasing revenues to $9 billion by 1996,
nylon business, assuming U.S. Federal Trade Commissic
apparel and carpet markets.

We continue to focus on three long-term strateg
high-volume fibers -- nylon and "Dacron" for appare
in cost, quality, service and innovation. An aggre
specialty businesses -- "Lycra" spandex, "Kevlar"
ites business, our strategy is to develop and po
materials, such as metals.

client
**e. i. du pont de
nemours and company**
design firm
frankfurt balkind partners
creative directors
aubrey balkind   kent hunter
designer
kin yuen
illustrator
holland
photographer
greg weiner

client
l g & e energy corp.
design firm
corporate reports inc.
art director/designer
brant day
illustrator
guy billout
photographers
john webb, quadrant
bill ray

LG&E Energy Corp.

Annual Report 1 9 9 3

Looking from the Outside In

Louisville Gas and Electric Company

Retail Electric

Helping Customers Grow Their Businesses

LG&E is customizing its retail services to meet individual customers' evolving needs. It is helping customers use electricity more strategically. And it is creating new, high-value electricity applications that enhance customers' core businesses.

For example, in 1993 LG&E worked with Ford's Kentucky Truck Plant to provide the additional electricity necessary for a $650 million expansion. Upon completion in 1995, the facility will be the world's largest truck assembly plant for medium- to heavy-sized trucks. It will enable Ford to increase its production from 24 to 45 trucks per hour. As a partner in Ford's growth, LG&E engineered access to a 69,000-volt power line, installed two transformers and constructed a substation on the plant premises. Through the cooperative effort, Ford increases production, LG&E increases revenues, and the community gains 1,400 new jobs.

Exploring Cost Efficiencies With Customers

LG&E customers currently benefit from some of the lowest-cost electric service in the country, with rates 27 percent below the national average. Still, LG&E is working closely with all of its customer groups to help them find ways to make the most of their energy usage.

LG&E consults with its major industrial customers to help them maintain maximum control over their energy usage. For example, industrial users can shift manufacturing to off-peak hours, opt for interruptible service or re-engineer processes to take advantage of cost-saving rate structures.

LG&E worked closely in 1993 with government leaders and consumer representatives to create the first demand-side management (DSM) initiative approved for an investor-owned utility by Kentucky's Public Service Commission. As part of this conservation effort, the company is authorized to decouple its sales from revenues. This removes the disincentive for utilities to aggressively pursue demand-side management goals.

LG&E's two-pronged strategy combines efficient use with low prices. This approach improves industrial customers' competitive edge and lowers residential customers' bills. When customers win, LG&E wins.

LG&E is always looking for new technology that provides high-value electricity applications for customers, such as LG&E's new radio-frequency automatic meter reading process.

Setting New Standards for Service

LG&E is continually looking for non-traditional approaches and new technology to serve customers more effectively.

In 1993 LG&E replaced more than 6,000 of its conventional electric and about 5,500 conventional gas meters with new radio-signaled meters. Under this program, a computer-equipped van driven by customers' houses and collects readings through radio waves from the meters. This system saves time and reduces LG&E's expenses for field personnel. It also enhances customer convenience and reduces the number of estimated bills.

Also in 1993 LG&E began preliminary discussions with local economic development

LG&E Retail Electric Sales by Customer Type
(Percent of kwh sales to ultimate consumers)
LG&E serves a wide variety of electric customers, balancing their diverse needs.

Other 17%
Residential 35%
Large Industrial 26%
Large Commercial 4%
Small Commercial and Industrial 11%

client
new mexico symphony orchestra
design firm
vaughn wedeen creative
art director
steve wedeen
designers
steve wedeen   dan slan

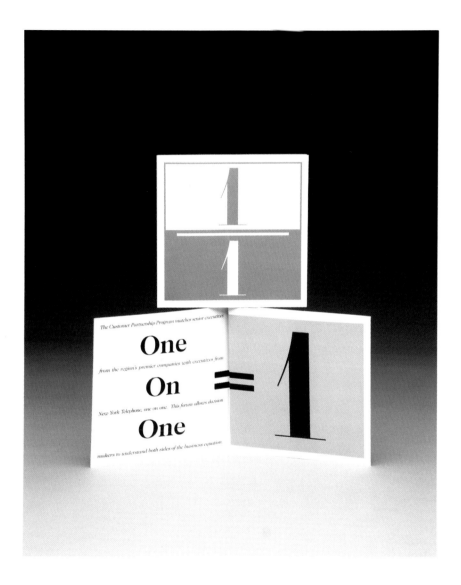

client
new york telephone
design firm
mike quon design office, inc.
creative director
mike quon
art director
teresa alpert
designers
mike quon   erick kuo

client
mohawk paper mills
design firm
mohawk paper mills
designers
michael bierut   lisa cerveny
dana arnett   p. scott makela
photographer
john paul endress

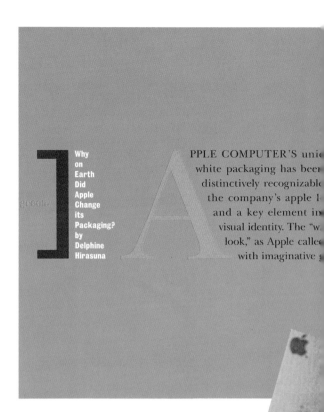

] Why
on
Earth
Did
Apple
Change
its
Packaging?
by
Delphine
Hirasuna

PPLE COMPUTER'S uni
white packaging has beer
distinctively recognizable
the company's apple l
and a key element in
visual identity. The "w
look," as Apple calle
with imaginative

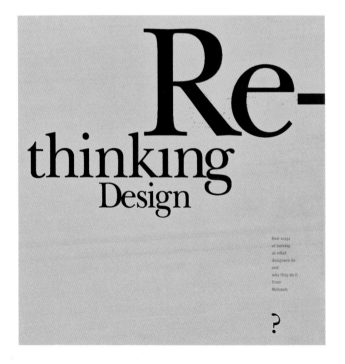

Re-
thinking
Design

How ways
of looking
at what
designers do
and
why they do it
from
Mohawk

?

Macir

...phics of a Macintosh, had helped ...position the "Mac" as a friendly, ...approachable computer. So, when ...Apple Computer switched from ...pristine white packaging to un-...bleached brown boxes using ...recycled fiber, it was not without ...trepidation. ● But the boxes'

client
simpson paper company
design firm
pentagram
creative director
woody pirtle
designers
woody pirtle   john klotnia
ivette montes de oca   ron louie

Japanese mythology attributes many natural
phenomena to family feuds among the gods.
    Amaterasu the sun goddess and her brother
Moon caused night and day because they sat
sulking in the celestial heavens with their backs
to one another. Amaterasu didn't like her
unruly little brother Susano the storm god
either. Susano once visited her domain, sup-
posedly to apologize for his past behavior, but
instead wreaked havoc on her rice fields.
The sun goddess angrily withdrew into a cave,
plummeting the world into darkness.
    To cajole her to come out, the minor gods
threw a lively party, even enticing roosters
to crow, and hung a huge mirror outside the
cave. Unable to resist the merriment, the sun
goddess emerged. Seeing her own radiance
reflected in the mirror, she happily restored
daylight to the world.

AUTUMN
BLUSH
COVER 80 LB.

EQUINOX

JAPANESE SUN GODDESS

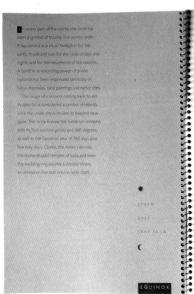

In every part of the world, the circle has
been a symbol of totality and cosmic order.
It has served as a visual metaphor for the
earth, moon and sun, for the cycle of days and
nights, and for the recurrence of the seasons.
A belief in an encircling power of divine
radiance has been expressed spiritually in
halos, mandalas, sand paintings and native rites.
    The image of a serpent circling back to eat
its own tail is considered a symbol of rebirth,
since the snake sheds its skin to become new
again. The circle framed the Sumerian compass
with its four cardinal points and 360 degrees,
as well as the Sumerian year of 360 days plus
five holy days. Clocks, the Aztec calendar,
the dome-shaped temples of India and even
the wedding ring assume a circular shape,
an unbroken line that returns unto itself.

STORM
GREY
TEXT 80 LB.

EQUINOX

client
international paper
design firm
liska and associates, inc.
art director
steve liska
designers
marcia lausen   heidi fleschko
photographer
laurie rubin

Six lightly fibered colors suggest less is more. It's easy to go natural.

COOL
UNDER
PRESSURE

CRUSHE

O WH

client
fox river/howard paper
design firm
sayles graphic design
art director/designer
john sayles
illustrator
john sayles

CRUSHED LEAF • O, WHAT A RELEAF

Cream, Smooth, 80# Cover.

WHAT A RELEAF

LEAF™

-A-RELEAF

client
elseware corporation
design firm
hornall anderson design works
art director/designer
jack anderson
designers
debra hampton   leo raymundo

client
agi, inc.
design firm
thirst
designer
rick valicenti
illustrator
thirst

client
western regional greek conference
design firm
sayles graphic design
art director/designer
john sayles
illustrator
john sayles

client
moore labels
design firm
gardner + greteman
art directors
bill gardner   sonia greteman
designer
bill gardner

client
coppola enterprises
design firm
mauck + associates
art director
kent mauck
designer
david jordan
photographer
andy lyons

environment

New Colors
New Duplexes
100% Recycled

ENVIRONMENT® Papers
for Writing, Text or Cover

Laser Compatible

Neenah Paper

client
neenah paper
design firm
em2 design
creative director
maxey andress
designer
mark nelson
photographer
chas underwood

Separating Color Photography:
Pre-press Issues for Printing on
Uncoated Paper

client
monadnock paper mills, inc.

design firm
chermayeff & geismar

creative director
tom geismar

designer
cathy schaefer

photographer
david arky photography

50/10 Matte allures

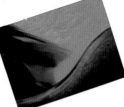

with a rich velvet

touch that seduces your

sensory vision.

50/10 Cream Matte

richest vision

client
mohawk paper mills
design firm
liska and associates, inc.
art director
steve liska
designer
kim nyberg

Mohawk 50/10

Vision

client
monadnock paper mills, inc.
design firm
weymouth design
creative director
michael weymouth
designer
tom kraft
photographers
susan segal   george petrakes
jeffrey titcomb   bruce rogovin
sanjay kothori   michael weymouth

client
vitra gmbh
design firm
mendell & oberer
designers
pierre mendell   klaus oberer
photographer
hans hansen

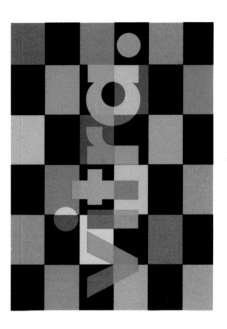

client
gilbert paper
design firm
sayles graphic design
art director/designer
john sayles
illustrator
john sayles

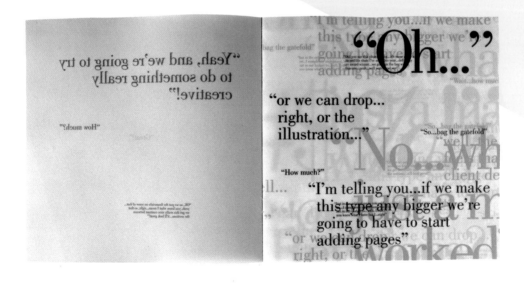

So you just found out you're designing next year's annual report.

"Oh..."

"or we can drop...
right, or the
illustration..."

"How much?"

"I'm telling you...if we make
this type any bigger we're
going to have to start
adding pages"

"Yeah, and we're going to try
to do something really
creative!"

"How much?"

client
mohawk paper mills
design firm
liska and associates, inc.
art director
steve liska
designer
kim nyberg

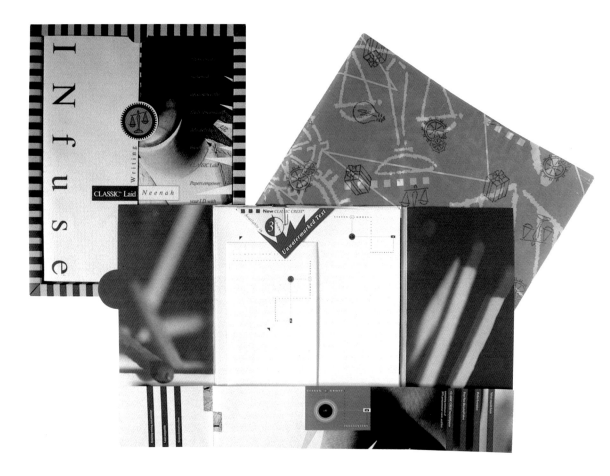

client
neenah paper
design firm
em2 design
creative director
maxey andress
designers
maxey andress   tamar akou
illustrator
clem bedwell
photographer
terri teague

client
kba planeta north america, inc.
design firm
fiorentino associates
creative director
lou fiorentino
designers
andy eng   sabrina wu

William H. Gass
Fiction and the Figures of Life

But the Popocatepetl of the novel is yet another mountain, and [has] quite a different function. Lowry is constructing a place describing one; he is making a Mexico for the mind where, strictly speaking, there are not menacing volcanoes, only menacing phrases, where complex chains of concepts traverse our consciousness, and where, unlike history, events take place in the moment that we read them — over and over as it may be, irregularly even, at widely separated times — whenever we restore these notes to music.

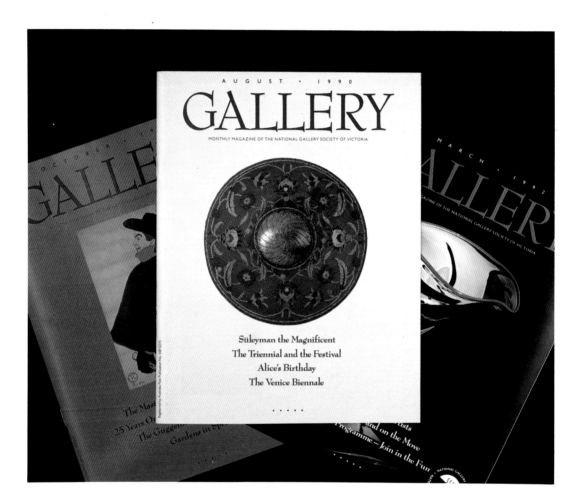

client
national gallery society of victoria
design firm
mamolitti chan design

When **folding**
coated paper, it
should be scored to
avoid cracking,
especially if it is laid
out against the grain
or the fold runs
through an area of
heavy ink coverage.
Any job with a
gatefold should be
scored at the thumb
edge to help prevent
cracking and to
make the job lie
flatter. Cover stock
should always be
scored, no matter
what the grain
direction. For best
results in scoring,
a letter-press
channel score
should be used.

SHOW QUALITY

client
consolidated papers, inc.
design firm
petrick design
designer
robert petrick
photographers
jean moss   jeff noble

EP **CASAD** 1994
world record holding water skis and equipment
catalog

client
wellington leisure

design firm
em2 design

art director
maxey andress

designer
mark silvers

photographers
doug dukane   deloris thrash

active wear

You do what you gotta do. Even if it hurts, I'm going to get that extra buoy. And believe me, sometimes it hurts.

Susi Graham
World record holder, many titled champion, first woman to clear 38 off. On being labeled "scrappy" by the sports press.

4a, 4b ANTRON® JACKET AND PANTS
Water-resistant outershell of 100% Antron® nylon fabric with crinkled finish. Jacket features yoke shoulder design with vented back. Slash front pockets featured on the pants. Machine washable.
Sizes: S, M, L, XL.

4c, 4d STRIPED BUTTON BASEBALL SHIRT AND COTTON KNIT SHORTS
Traditional baseball styling in ash with black pinstriping. Shirt features six button front and fishtail bottom. Shorts feature covered elastic waistband. Double needle stitching, 100% combed cotton.
Sizes: S, M, L, XL.

Back of dude
Wearing a heavyweight tee-shirt and striped cotton knit shorts. Made for dudettes too.

4e PLAID FLANNEL SHORTS
True yarn dyed cotton flannel, two side pockets, covered elastic waistband, 100% cotton.
Sizes: S, M, L, XL.

4f, 4g HEAVYWEIGHT TEE-SHIRT AND SHORTS W/POCKETS
Full athletic cut, set-in collar, taped shoulder-to-shoulder, 100% compacted-cotton jersey. Shorts feature long baggy cut, side pockets, covered elastic waistband, inside waist drawstring and double needle hem.
Sizes: S, M, L, XL.
Shorts: S, M, L, XL.

4h LONG SLEEVE MOCK TEE
Garment dyed 100% cotton jersey, oversize cut, rib knit mock turtleneck, long sleeves with rib cuffs.
Sizes: L, XL.

4i SHORT SLEEVE MOCK TEE
Garment dyed 100% cotton jersey. Shirt features oversize cut, rib knit turtleneck and hemmed sleeves.
Sizes: Shirt: L, XL.

4j BASEBALL CAP

EP **CASAD**
world record holding water skis and equipment
1994

exceptional
Performance:
on the water
in the showroom
and from the
company.

client
du pont
design firm
mike quon design office, inc.
creative director
mike quon
designers
mike quon   eileen kinneary

client
neenah paper
design firm
copeland hirthler
design + communication
creative director
brad copeland
designer
suzy miller

CLASSIC™ Laid Writing

Rich in depth, texture and feel, CLASSIC™ Laid is unmatched by any premium correspondence offering. Rediscover CLASSIC Laid with its new palette of artistry, featuring: twelve recycled colors, "brushed" and "peppered" tones plus additional laser compatible items. All masterfully executed in a variety of weights.

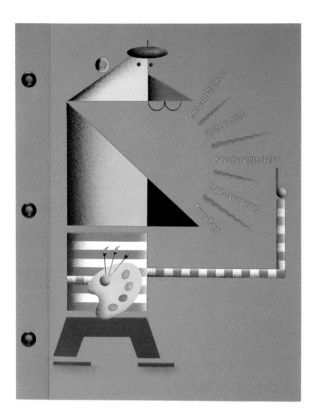

client
black book marketing group
design firm
mcdaniel design inc.
art director
lori h. mcdaniel
designer
benedict turner

FIRST YOU HAVE TO BE SEEN...

Art directors use every conceivable tool to find talent. They look at magazines, books, direct mail, collateral, and when they have time, they see portfolios.

Mostly, however, they don't have time. That's why The Creative Illustration Book has become the most effective way to be seen nationally by illustration buyers.

Art directors know that when they pick up CIB they'll see work on a par with the finest awards annuals. Established stars and exciting new talent. Plus a broad variety of styles.

Yet CIB is not a phone book. It does not bury illustrators or test the physique of art directors. The book is hardbound, for durability and ease of use. And it's published by the company that invented creative directories twenty-two years ago: The Creative Black Book.

The basic philosophy of CIB comes down to quality: of the work it contains, of design, production and distribution. The result of this quality is a book that's shipped to the art directors who give you work. A book art directors use again and again because it helps solve creative problems quickly and expertly.

CIB may not let you retire to Tahiti, at least not immediately. But it will open the right doors, position you among the top talent, and give you the benefit of The Black Book's marketing expertise. The rest is up to you.

CREATIVE

ILLUSTRATION

BOOK

client
graphic arts center
design firm
pentagram design, inc.
art director
kit hinrichs
designer
belle how
illustrators
dan picaso   will nelson
photography
barry robinson   terry hefferman
gary braasch   steven bloch
portland art museum

NO
YES

client
the bradley printing company
design firm
liska and associates, inc.
art director
steve liska
designer
richard taylor
photographer
scott morgan

client
neenah paper
design firm
em2 design
creative director
maxey andress
designer
tamar akou
illustrator
em2 design
photographer
chas studio

client
philip morris
design firm
mike quon design office, inc.
creative director
mike quon
designer
erick kuo

...SINESS SKILLS TO

...USA introduced
...romotion event in
...s on each specially
...redeemable for
...enture Team Gear.
...puter will calculate
...o Adventure Team
...ermarkets nationwide
...omotion on January 4th,
...MI on May 12.

...sest to the computer will win
...venture Team 4x4. Runners-up, as
...ticipants, will receive valuable prizes.

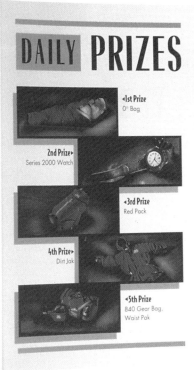

DAILY PRIZES

◄**1st Prize**
0° Bag

2nd Prize►
Series 2000 Watch

◄**3rd Prize**
Red Pack

4th Prize►
Dirt Jak

◄**5th Prize**
B40 Gear Bag,
Waist Pak

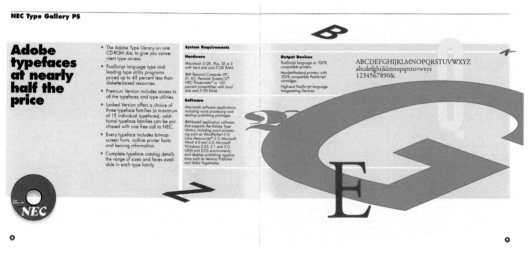

client
nec technologies, inc

design firm
liska and associates, inc.

art director
steve liska

designer
brock haldeman

client
potlatch corporation
design firm
liska and associates, inc.
art director
steve liska
designer
anne schedler

client
national travelers life
design firm
sayles graphic design
art director/designer
john sayles
photographer
comstock

client
lithographix & butler paper
design firm
louey/rubino design group inc.
creative director
robert louey
art director
regina rubino
designers
robert louey   regina rubino
illustrator
ayse ulay
photographer
gabor ekecs

At first glance, you may admire the
many techniques of advanced electronic
image enhancement displayed in these
shots... There's merging, cloning,
cutting and pasting, rotating, resizing,
masking, retouching and colour
balancing, for a start.

But that's just the beginning...
All of these techniques – and more –
are available through **Lumière**.
BGM's dynamic new image enhancement
service. And while the techniques
themselves are not new **Lumière** is –
and it casts image enhancement in a
new light. You'll begin to see what we
mean when you take a closer look.

FROM THE IMPRESSIVE FIRST GLANCE...

BGM COLOUR LABORATORIES LIMITED

ELECTRONIC IMAGE ENHANCEMENT IN A NEW LIGHT

BGM
BGM Colour Laboratories Limited

client
bgm colour laboratories limited
design firm
eskind waddell
photography
the image bank of canada
masterfile corporation

If you look very closely, you'll see one of the features that sets **Lumière** apart. Spectacular resolution. Look at these prints with a magnifying glass. The resolution quality you see is made possible by the fact that **Lumière** produces images on continuous tone photographic negatives and transparencies. And that is the ultimate image enhancement.

So look closely at these prints—and then look beyond them.

With this kind of resolution, you can imagine the possibilities. Start with multi-purpose photo applications in retail advertising — for point-of-sale and sales promotion materials... and for display media, including large format murals and posters, reflective or backlit. And then

consider the possibilities of this kind of quality for pre-press and other communications media... **Lumière** opens up a new range of applications. And there's much more to it than meets the eye.

...ZLING CLOSER LOOK...

Lumière is much more than an electronic system... much more than the sophisticated hardware and software, the scanning technology, the workstations, and the outstanding image display of our monitors. **Lumière** is a service — a BGM service - which is designed to get unparalleled results from the image enhancement process.

Lumière includes full service consultation with our expert staff, who are dedicated to working closely with clients; it involves our highly creative and skilled operators, who know how to weave images together seamlessly. It accesses our broad range of photo reproduction services... and it draws on the expertise of Canada's leading colour lab — BGM — where we know how to make the most of your image.

So whether you're a photo designer... a creative director... a marketing executive... or anyone involved in the assembly and display of images; we'd like to put you in the picture, and show you what **Lumièr** can do for you — so that you can start imagining what you can do with **Lumière**.

THERE'S MORE TO **LUMIÈRE** THAN MEETS THE EYE...

Lumière

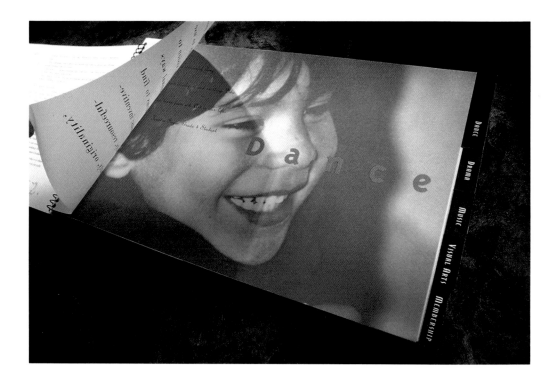

client
**the music center of
los angeles county**
design firm
maureen erbe design
art director
maureen erbe
designers
maureen erbe   rita sowins

client
western regional greek conference
design firm
sayles graphic design
art director/designer
john sayles
illustrator
john sayles

client
cleveland institute of art
design firm
nesnadny + schwartz
creative directors
joyce nesnadny   mark schwartz
designers
joyce nesnadny   brian lavy
photographers
mark schwartz   robert a. muller

1993~1994

Cleveland **Institute of Art** a professional college of art and design

Our approach is holistic. Schedules list separate courses, but our cooperative

teaching style diffuses the borders between these courses. Teaching here is

than one-directional, teacher-to-student. There is a friendly exchange

s, among faculty, and between students and faculty. Rob Jergens

15

Ceramics
18
Enameling
22
Glass
26
Illustration
30
Interior Design
34   Medical Illustration
Metals
38
Photography
42
Sculpture

Drawin
2
Fiber
24
Graphic Design
Industrial Design
28
32
Medical Illustration
36
Painting
Printmaking
40
44

client
converse
design firm
houston effler & partners
creative directors
rich herstek   **peter favat**
art director
monica taylor
designers
monica taylor   **glenn kennedy**
photographers
hiro   **andy parsons**

DON'T WADE INTO THE MAINSTREAM.

RETAILER NAME

client
southern california edison
design firm
white design
art director
john white
designer
aram youssefian
illustrators
aram youssefian
maxine mueller

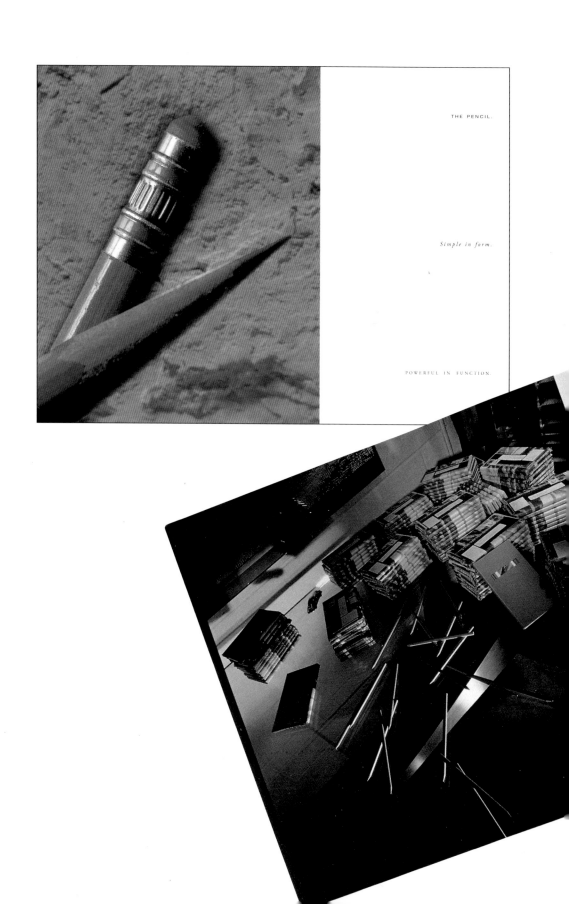

THE PENCIL.

Simple in form.

POWERFUL IN FUNCTION.

client
d.z. communications
design firm
d.z. communications
creative director/art director
don zubalsky
illustrators
**istvan banyai   joel nakamura
mike quon**
photographers
**caesar lima   eshel ezer
e.k. waller**

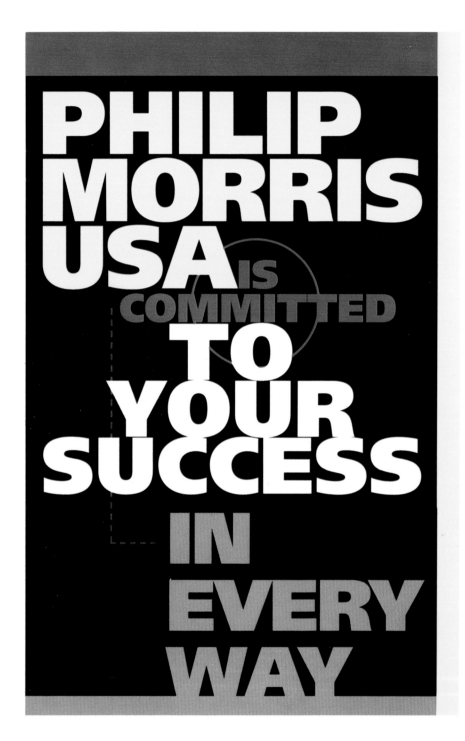

client
philip morris
design firm
mike quon design office, inc.
creative director
mike quon
designer
erick kuo

client
details, member steelcase
design partnership
design firm
doublespace
art directors
david sterling   monica halpert
jane kosstrin
designer
klaus kempenaars
photographer
elliott kaufman

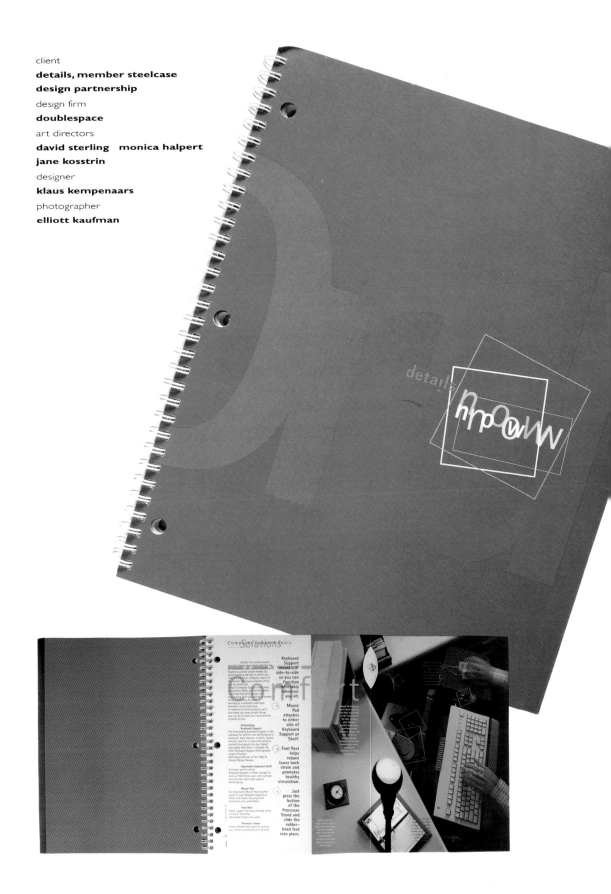

client
greenleaf medical
design firm
earl gee design
art director/designer
earl gee
photographer
geoffrey nelson

client
champion international
design firm
alexander isley design
art director
alexander isley
designer
lynette cortez
illustrator
sergio baradat

Nusrat Ali Fatah Khan was up there on stage, a huge pyramid of a man, a fat singing buddha with hair. The band, a few percussionists, a harmonium player and some singers, were there to spur him on, and they did a good job. Phrase after phrase of his pealed above the accompaniment and the intensity of the performance grew and grew. Pakistanis in the balcony were standing up, eyes rolling back into their heads, moaning, hands up in the air. A stream of people were coming up to the stage, tossing handfuls of money towards the band, and oddly, men were coming up to make change with what was on stage, then throwing what they wanted at him and the band. He was singing reli- gious music, meant to make people go into a trance that brought them closer to God. It worked. The near repetitions of the music, where each new phrase had something to do with the previous one, brought the audience to a heightened state, involving them intellectually while the endlessness of the variations and the athleticism of the performances moved people emotionally. The sheer excellence of it, the unadulturated religiosity of it, was a tribute to purity. There is nothing pure but personal experience, and at that special moment, everyone in the audience understood the same thing, that the music was uncorruptible.

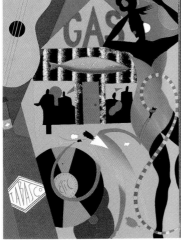

stretched the side of the club, which was about 50 or so yards long. The bartenders were women, fat and ugly, with beehive hair- dos, and lines like "Honey, you can ride this home anytime." The club drew from the black com- munity, men who worked on fish boats and in fish processing factories; they couldn't get rid of the smell of fish from their skin and only spoke creole French. The women worked as nurses, or stayed home, and when people went to the club they went to spend their money. The music started promptly at 10 and smiled when the sun came up. Joe Hicks and his Playhell Playboys alternated with Les Frères Charle, bands that rocked and rolled, using a mixture of French country music, learned from the Arcadian settlers of southwestern Louisiana, and the leftover black and Indian music, along with black rhythm and blues. It was an inviting place; white people

weren't strangers there. You just paid your $6 and went off in. Somewhere after midnight the place completely changed. People stopped coming in, and nobody left. Everybody danced, and the dance floor crammed up, women started throwing their hands up in the air and ejaculating. An hour later, the ecstatic moments had swept through the crowd. The music, driving away on just a rickety chord or two, pounded this club, the rattle of the washboard locked in tight with the bands' drum- mers, the occasional vocal breaking up the long, hard-driving instrumental sections. By the time it was over, a sort of communal ecstasy had been reached, and people wandered out into the sunlight, purged and ready for Sunday, and the rest of the week.

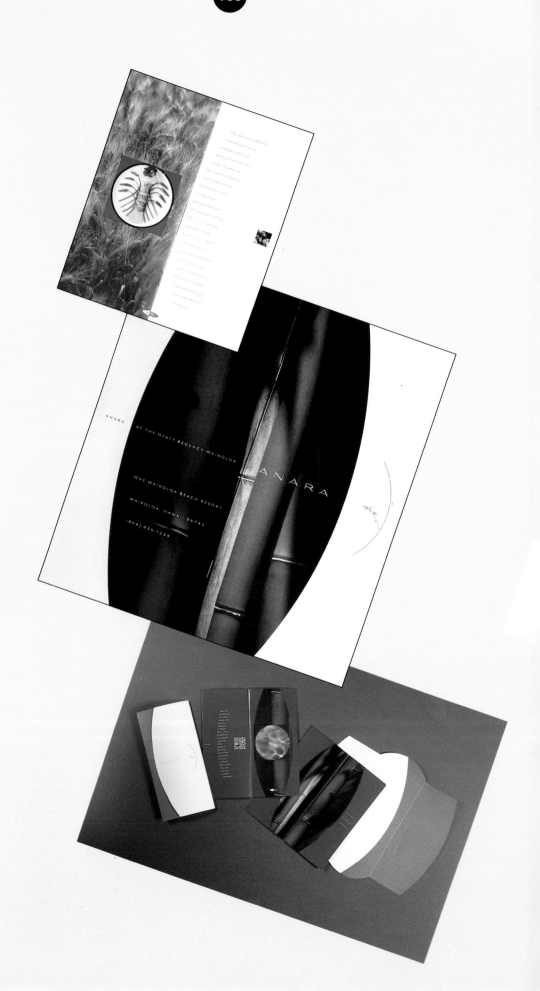

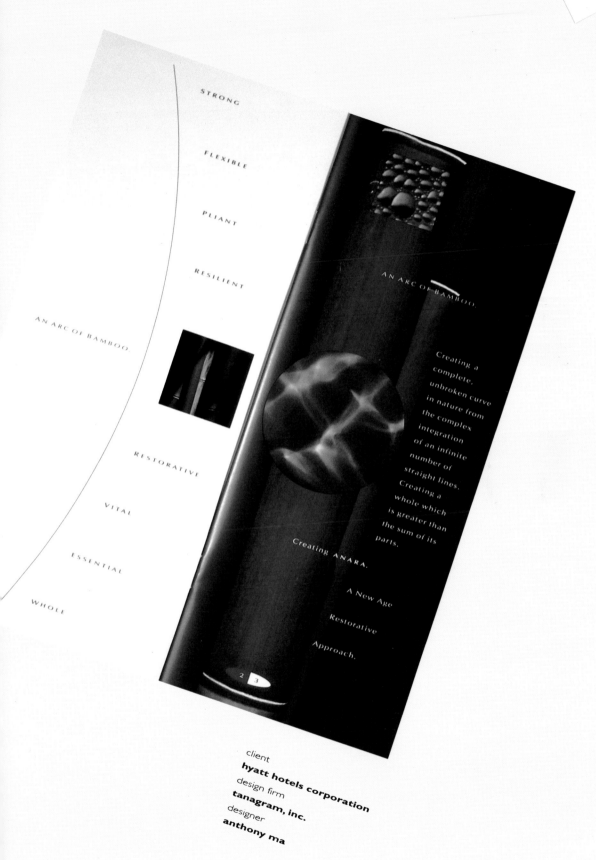

STRONG

FLEXIBLE

PLIANT

RESILIENT

AN ARC OF BAMBOO.

RESTORATIVE

VITAL

ESSENTIAL

WHOLE

AN ARC OF BAMBOO.

Creating a
complete,
unbroken curve
in nature from
the complex
integration
of an infinite
number of
straight lines.
Creating a
whole which
is greater than
the sum of its
parts.

Creating ANARA.

A New Age

Restorative

Approach.

2 3

client
hyatt hotels corporation
design firm
tanagram, inc.
designer
anthony ma

client
corning inc.
design firm
**corning inc., corporate
design department**
designers
**william s. lucas
jennifer elsenfeld**
illustrator
mike quon

client
troxel cycling and fitness, inc.
design firm
the kottler caldera group
art director
bart welch
photographer
bob carey photography

client
lunar design
design firm
michael mabry design
designers/illustrators
michael mabry   peter soe

LUNAR

client
annieglass
design firm
russel leong design
art director
russel k. leong
designers
russel k. leong   pam m. matsuda
betsy todd
photographer
r. j. muna

More durable than fine
china. Nuances in each
plate are created by the
artist's brushstroke.
Crafted in thick glass.
Hand-painted with
24K gold and platinum.
Kiln fired for durability
and strength. Chip and
scratch resistant.

13

client
mtv networks
design firm
frankfurt balkind partners
creative directors
aubrey balkind   kent hunter
designers/illustrators
johan vipper   andreas combüchen

client
museum of natural history

design firm
mike quon design office, inc.

creative director
mike quon

art director
gro frivoll

client
butler paper
design firm
louey/rubino design group inc.
creative director
robert louey
art director
regina rubino
designers
robert louey   regina rubino
illustrator
joel nakamura
photographers
bard martin   burton pritz

client
neenah paper
design firm
copeland hirthler
design & communication
art director/designer
suzy miller
illustrator
suzy miller

client
head golf
design firm
rbmm/the richards group
art director
d. c. stipp
designers
d. c. stipp   janet cowling
photographers
neal farris   jim olvera

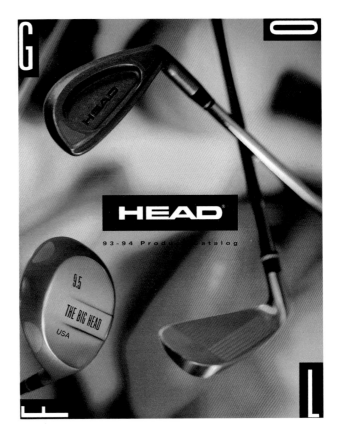

HUNTERS FISHERMEN GOLFERS SKIERS YACHTSMEN 20,000,000 STRONG MEN YOU CAN COUNT ON

TIMES MIRROR MAGAZINE NETWORK

client
times mirror magazine network
design firm
mc studio/times mirror magazines
creative director
paul kelly
art director
monica gotz
illustrator
douglas fraser
photography
sean smith
fpg stock photography
superstock masterfile

Men who fish.
Men who hunt.
Men who sail.
Men who build.
Men who ski.
Men who golf.

Men who invest.
Men who relax.
Men who wine.
Men who dine.
Men who travel.
Men who acquire.

client
**institute for biological
research and devlopement**
design firm
jann church partners, inc.
designer
jann church

client
etonic
design firm
clarke goward
art director
marc gallucci
photographers
john goodman
bill miles

Women's Trans Am

Trans Am Trainer

Designed with our patented Dr. McGregor Heel & Arch Support.®
this is a classic running shoe designed for exceptional fit with width-sizing comfort and cushioning.
Features a solid rubber outsole and split suede or leather and polyjag upper.

Women's Sizes: AA 6–10, B 5–10, 11, D 6 · 10
ER6005   White/Light Grey (suede/polyjag)
ER6600   White/Light Grey (leather/polyjag)
Women's Sizes: B 5–10, 11
ER6009   White/Cyan Blue (not shown)

Trans Am Leather

The same shoe as our classic Trans Am Trainer, but this model features an upper of full grain leather.

Women's Sizes: B 5–10, 11, D 6–10
K390   White/Light Grey
Women's Sizes: B 5–10
K392   Black

W a l k i n g

14

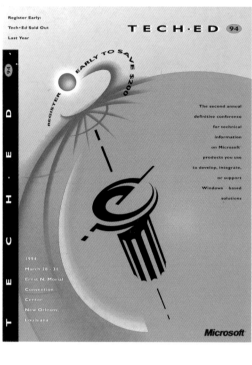

client
microsoft corporation
design firm
hornall anderson design works
art director
jack anderson
designers
jack anderson   cliff chung
leslie macinnes   david bates
illustrator
steve coppin

client
leo's dancewear
design firm
nicholas associates
art director
nicholas sinadinos
designers
nicholas sinadinos   christine simpson
photographer
art ketchum

client
argus
design firm
segura inc.
designer
carlos segura
photographer
montressor

client
genfoot, inc.
design firm
midnight oil studios
creative director
kathryn klein
design director
james skiles
illustrators
tim mcgrath   chris elliot
midnight oil studios
photography
john van s., boston
fpg stock photography

Keep an eye out ...

Listen for details on...

...approach to state-of-the-art imaging.

Brain, spine, knee, the
abdomen. No matter
or complex the proc
our GE Signa 1.5 te
we're ready to han
MRI needs

NMR takes a hands on...

client
mid rockland imaging
design firm
mike quon design office, inc.
creative director
mike quon
designers
mike quon   erick kuo

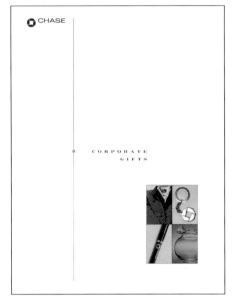

CORPORATE
GIFTS

client
the chase manhattan bank
design firm
mcdaniel design, inc.
art director/designer
lori h. mcdaniel
designer
janwalai kusuwan
photographer
taka photography nyc

client
beckett paper
design firm
scott hull + associates
art directors/designers
marcia gabor   steve gabor
photographer
greg dearth

A Week in the Mountains.

client
plainclothes
design firm
slaughter/hanson
creative director
terry slaughter
designer/illustrator
marion english
photographer
ed thomas

client
beckett paper
design firms
northlich stolley lawarre
lamson design
art directors
john stryker   dale lamson
designers
dale lamson   david mill
illustrator
jim effler/air studio
photography
peggy mchale
stock photography

client
plainclothes
design firm
slaughter/hanson
art director/designer
marion english
photographer
rick hornlick

client
polytrade corporation
design firm
tommy li design ltd.
art director
tommy li
designers
william ho
chin-lee ma
photographers
philip wong   chester ong
ossert lam   lee ka sing
chan chun nam   wher law
michael lee   stephen cheung
ringo tang

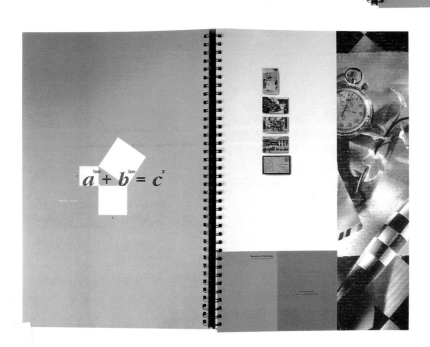

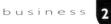
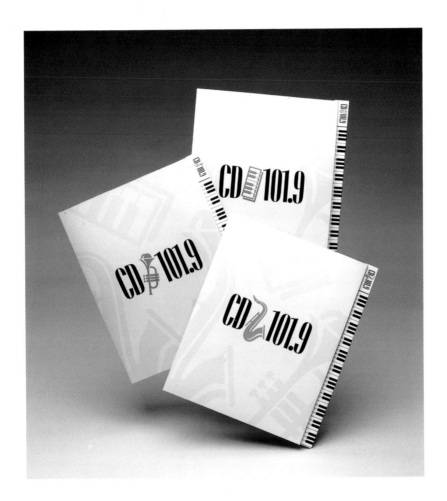

client
wqcd-fm, nyc
design firm
mike quon design office, inc.
creative directors
dale pon   mike quon
designer
eileen kinneary
illustrator
sam gunn

client
sidney printing works
design firm
siebert design associates
art director
lori siebert
designers
lori siebert   lisa ballard
photographer
jeff friedman

client
how design conference
design firm
segura inc.
designer
carlos segura

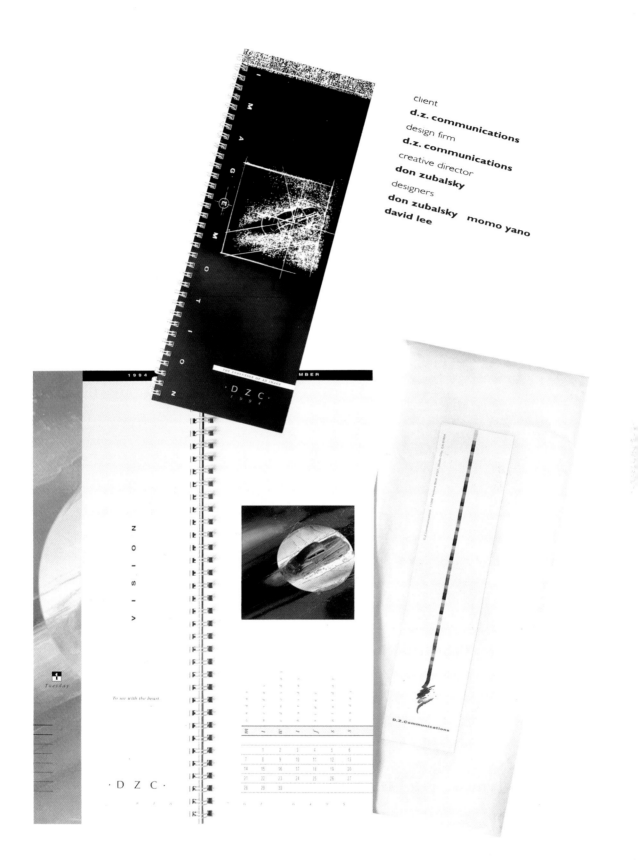

client
d.z. communications
design firm
d.z. communications
creative director
don zubalsky
designers
don zubalsky   momo yano
david lee

client
specialized bicycles
design firm
lisa levin design
art director/designer
lisa levin
photographers
tim davis   michael venera

client
komoto international
design firm
jann church partners, inc.
designer
jann church

client
converse
design firm
houston effler & partners
art directors/designers
monica taylor   jawbone productions
photographer
andy parsons photography

22 THE PYRAMID AT LE GRAND LOUVRE
copywriter **charles f. donnelly**
printer **teagle & little, norfolk, virginia**
paper stock **repap lithofectplus®** *(recycled coated paper)*

23 THE FACE OF RECYCLING BROCHURE
copywriter **delphine hirasuna**
printer **graphic arts center, portland, oregon**
print run **45,000**
printing technique **four-color process and match colors**
paper stock **sundance, gainsborough, coronado, equinox, quest, evergreen**
design/prepress **traditional**

24 FRONTIER FOLDER & INSERTS
copywriter **james burke**
printer **pearl pressman liberty, philadelphia, pennsylvania**
print run **3,000** *(large folders),* **6,000** *(small folders),* **2,000** *(inserts)*
printing technique **four-color process and one pms, die-cut**
paper stock **hammermill opaque recycled**
design/prepress **macintosh quadra 700** *(aldus freehand, adobe photoshop)*
budget **$25,000**

This folder and inserts program plays off the company's name, highlights cutting-edge technology, and can be modified with custom inserts. Wasted space on the press sheet was utilized to run 4" x 9" folders, two-up. This allowed the client's secondary sales vehicle to be mailed in a No. 10 envelope.

26 IDS WORKPLACE DESIGN/PRODUCTION BROCHURE
copywriter **joni spencer**
production manager **april cummings**
printer **hillsboro printing, tampa, florida**
print run **5,000**
printing technique **four-color process and one pms** *(text),* **four-color process, one side** *(overlay sheets)*
paper stock **confetti kaleidoscope 80# canson satin** *(cover)*
design/prepress **macintosh** *(quark xpress, adobe illustrator, adobe photoshop)*
budget **$52,300**

To show that IDS designs for productivity and a healthier office environment, a well-designed workplace was compared to the efficient design of a beehive. The brochure was packed in a handmade wooden box with a jar of IDS "Success is Sweet" honey and delivered to key corporate prospects. Many of the photographic images were silhouetted, airbrushed and stripped electronically on Scitex and blaze software.

26 NICHOLS INSTITUTE FACILITY BROCHURE
printer **woods lithographix, phoenix, arizona**
print run **10,000**
printing technique **200 line four-color process, metallic inks**
paper stock **quintessence**
design/prepress **traditional**

This direct mail brochure was used to inform and inspire positive public opinion regarding new site location for Nichols Institute.

27 TECHNOLOGY ASSESSMENT
printer **first impression, elk grove village, illinois**
print run **1,000**
printing technique **two pms**
paper stock **reflections**
design/prepress **macintosh quadra 840** *(quark xpress)*

The diagrammatic format presents the division of the Andersen Consulting group in a tangible and accessible way to clients and partners.

28 CENTURA PAPER PROMOTION
printer **lake county press, waukegan, illinois**
printing technique **four-color process with overall aqueous coating**
paper stock **consolidated centura gloss** *(cover, text)*
design/prepress **traditional and macintosh** *(aldus freehand)*

A theme of "Light and Shadow" presented in a graphically and photographically rich design portrays how inks print on a specific paper line of Centura.

29 MULTIFECT® FROM REPAP
copywriter **charles f. donnelly**
printer **the hennegan company, cincinnati, ohio**
printing technique **175 line four-color process, gloss and dull varnishes, duotones and quadratones on a six-color heidelberg press**
paper stock **repap multifect®**

A variety of printing techniques was used to demonstrate the high performance level of Repap's Multifect, especially for a coated stock.

30 SUNCRAFT DIRECT MAIL BROCHURE
printer **graphic ads, atlanta, georgia**
print run **20,000**
printing technique **four-color process**
paper stock **consolidated futura dull, neenah uv**
design/prepress **macintosh quadra 950** *(quark xpress, adobe photoshop)*
budget **$50,000**

A Matisse-like color scheme was used in the photography for a more esoteric marketing approach.

32 GILBERT PAPER PROMOTION
copywriter **todd lief**
printer **d.l. terwilliger sterling-roman lithographers, new york, new york**
print run **20,000**
printing technique **four-color process, die-cut and channel scored**
paper stock **gilbert oxford white 80#** *(cover, text)*
design/prepress **macintosh ii ci** *(quark xpress, adobe illustrator, adobe photoshop)*
budget **$50,000**

33 MOBIUM CAPABILITIES BROCHURE
director of editorial services **dawn williams**
printer **columbia, chicago, illinois**
print run **1,000**
printing technique **offset silk screen**
paper stock **french speckletone, centura gloss, mega** *(wyndstone japanese collection)*
design/prepress
traditional and macintosh quadra 950 *(quark xpress, adobe illustrator, adobe photoshop)*
budget
$80,000

The interplay of words and images in a problem/solution format communicates Mobium's capabilities within current communication trends.

34 MCGRAW-HILL MANAGEMENT BROCHURE
printer **mcgraw-hill, inc.**
design/prepress **computer** *(aldus pagemaker)*

This brochure introduced updated management texts and supplementary materials to college management professors.

34 PHOBIA PROMOTIONAL PIECE
printer **westland printers, burtonsville, maryland**
print run **1,000**
printing technique **four-color process and varnish**
paper stock **vintage gloss**
design/prepress **traditional**
budget **$3,500**

Accompanied by a letter, this self-promotional piece for a marketing communications firm shows how strong, bold images can be used to make clients stand out from their competition.

35 PROCESS/1: SOFTWARE CAPABILITIES BROCHURE
printer **bradley printing, chicago, illinois**
paper stock **quintessence remark**
design/prepress **macintosh** *(quark xpress, aldus freehand, adobe photoshop)*

This brochure uses imagery that illustrates subject matter specific to process manufacturers to market software and educate clientele.

36 NEOCON92 "FURNISH YOUR MIND"
copywriters **alan gandelman, gary nuel**
printer **the argus press, niles, illinois**
print run **49,000**
printing technique **four-color process**
paper stock **consort royal silk and others**
design/prepress **macintosh ii ci**
budget **$30,000**

This brochure was used to inform and attract new attendies for the NeoCon92 interiors and furnishings show.

37 RESIDENTIAL REBATE PROGRAM
printer **monarch litho, montebello, california**
paper stock **simpson quest 80# white** *(cover, text)*
design/prepress **traditional and macintosh iici** *(quark xpress)*

To encourage Edison customers to purchase energy-efficient appliances and illustrate the scope of the project, this brochure uses a warm, earth-tone palette, recycled paper, and a new logo.

38 ACS CAPABILITIES/SALES BROCHURE
copywriter **lindsay beaman**
printer **woods lithographix, phoenix, arizona**
print run **3,500**
printing technique **tritone black and white photography, fifth and sixth colors were dry pass metallics, dry pass dull varnish over in-line gloss varnish**
paper stock **curtis tweedweave** *(cover),* **simpson quest** *(fly),* **potlatch** *(text)*
design/prepress **macintosh** *(quark xpress, adobe illustrator)*
budget **$35,000**

39 CONSOLIDATED REFLECTIONS II
printer **bruce offset, elk grove village, illinois**
print run **80,000**
printing technique **four-color process and two match metallics**
paper stock **reflections ii basis 85#/110#** *(cover, text)*
design/prepress **macintosh** *(quark xpress)*

40 NEOCON92
copywriter **alan gandelman**
printer **the argus press, niles, illinois**
print run **40,000**
printing technique **5/5**
paper stock **vintage velvet**
design/prepress **macintosh quadra 800**

42 *IS & IS BROCHURE*
copywriter **stan smith**
printer **lithographix, los angeles, california**
print run **5,000**
printing technique **six-color process and gloss/dull varnish with spot uv coating**
paper stock **consolidated reflections 100#/110#** *(cover, text)*
design/prepress **macintosh ii ci** *(aldus pagemaker)*

Distributed at trade shows, through direct mail, and 800 number channels, this brochure introduced TRW's IS & IS business unit to manufacturers and government agencies. All photography was done with a 4x5 camera with a Sinar digitally-controlled shutter.

44 *THE CHRONICLE OF POPULAR CULTURE*
printer **enterprise**
print run **10,000**
printing technique **four-color process**
paper stock **french speckletone**
design/prepress **computer** *(quark xpress)*
budget **$20,000**

This brochure was used to sell advertising in Entertainment Weekly. A python swallowing two generations represents the two consecutive generations (Baby Boomer and Gernation X) who read Entertainment Weekly.

46 *VISIONARY ONE: THE DEEMS CONSULTANCY*
printer **l & c ficks, chicago, illinois**
print run **5,000** *(identity),* **2,000** *(brochures)*
paper stock **curtis tuscan terra astroparch** *(identity),* **esse** *(brochure)*
design/prepress **macintosh** *(aldus freehand, adobe photoshop)*

In creating a manifesto and identity for a consultancy dealing with film directors, the design team used a more abstract approach since the clientele leans toward a visual understanding.

47 *WOVEN LEGENDS RESTORATION BROCHURE*
copywriter **george jeuremovic**
printer **oriental rug review, new hampton, new hampshire**
print run **10,000**
printing technique **four-color process**
paper stock **loe**
design/prepress **traditional and quadra 700** *(aldus pagemaker)*
budget **$10,000-15,000**

Two-page spreads highlight each selling point of Woven Legends Restoration's services with before and after photos, site photos, and descriptive words used as image.

48 *MERIDIAN PACIFIC CAPABILITIES BROCHURE*
printer **costello brothers lithographers, alhambra, california**
print run **7,000**
printing technique **four-color process, second hit of black and spot gloss varnish**
paper stock **karmamatte 80# white** *(cover)*
design/prepress **traditional**
budget **$12,000 plus printing**

To demonstrate that Meridian Pacific is client oriented, and not transaction oriented, an illustrator was hired to graphically depict the headline "When square peg solutions won't do."

50 *INCENTIVE 100 BROCHURE*
copywriter **dan conaway**
typesetter **vineet thapar**
account manager **bill carkeet**
printer **lithograph printing, memphis, tennessee**
print run **40,000**
paper stock **international paper incentive 100**
design/prepress **macintosh quadra 950** *(quark xpress, adobe illustrator, adobe photoshop)*
budget **$200,000**

This brochure was part of a comprehensive marketing program introducing the industry's first 100 percent recycled offset paper made from de-inked newpapers and magazines.

51 *ARCHITEXTURE BROCHURE*
production **steven newman**
design/prepress **macintosh** *(quark xpress)*

52 *EDUCATION IS KNOWLEDGE CAMPAIGN*
computer production **chip wyly**
printer **frederic printing, denver, colorado**
print run **20,000**
printing technique **four-color process with aqueous coating**
paper stock **warren vintage gloss 100# book** *(brochure),* **potlach quintessence dull 100# text** *(poster),* **warren lustro saxony offset embossed 100# cover** *(folder)*
design/prepress **macintosh iicx** *(quark xpress, aldus freehand, adobe photoshop)*

54 *SELF-PROMOTION BROCHURE*
printer **burmeister lithography**
print run **3,500**
printing technique **four-color process and spot varnish on photos**
paper stock **mohawk perfect white** *(gatefold),* **potlatch mountie matte**
design/prepress **quadra 650** *(quark xpress, abobe illustrator, adobe photoshop)*
budget **$12,500**

55 *CARNEGIE HALL BROCHURE*
printer **lebanon valley offset**
print run **225,000**
printing technique **four-color process and gloss/dull varnish, quadratones**
paper stock **warren lustro gloss/dull cream**
design/prepress **traditional**

Carnegie Hall was chosen as the subject of this brochure for a symbol of creativity and high standards to promote S.D. Warren's paper line.

56 *CAPABILITIES BROCHURE*
printer **george rice & sons, seattle, washington**
print run **5,000**
printing technique **b/w and metallic in mid-tones, dull varnish in shadows** *(photos),* **multi-level emboss on cover**
paper stock **starwhite vicksburg** *(cover),* **starwhite lustrodull white** *(text)*
design/prepress **macintosh iici** *(aldus pagemaker)*

This system of brochures uses general photos to support the key strengths of Metlife's programs. Illustrations show specific areas of expertise.

58 *HECK BROCHURE*
printer **the argus press, niles, illinois**
print run **3,000**
paper stock **wyndstone consort royal silk**
design/prepress **quadra 800**
budget **$10,000**

60 *THE "H" WORD*
project manager **ted riley**
production **craig schommer**
printer **wall/peterson, minneapolis, minnesota**
print run **35,000**
printing technique **four-color process, one pms and matte varnish over five pms and spot varnish**
paper stock **cross pointe halopaque satin/vellum finish** *(cover, text, fly paper)*

To reinforce its unusual brand name, Halopaque was associated with other words with the same three letters. The brochure provides printing tips and comparative printing demonstrations on the various weights, colors and finishes of the paper.

61 *CAPABILITIES BROCHURE*
copywriter **russ haan**
printer **heritage graphics, phoenix, arizona**
print run **2,500**
printing technique **200 line four-color process and one pms touch plate on match photo**
paper stock **potlatch elequance gloss 85#** *(cover)*
design/prepress **macintosh quadra 900** *(quark xpress, adobe illustrator)*
budget **$17,000 plus printing**

62 *U.S. SAVINGS BONDS 1994 CAMPAIGN BROCHURE*
printer **george rice & sons, los angeles, california**
print run **30,000**
paper stock **gilbert esse 80# white** *(cover),* **warren lustro 80# enamel dull** *(text),* **gilbert esse 80# white green** *(text)*
design/prepress **computer** *(quark xpress)*

The variety of photographic images of America presented in this brochure creates a gallery of unique and diverse "visions." By encouraging viewers to reflect upon their own futures, these "visions" promote the purchase of US savings bonds.

63 *WHAT ARE THE QUESTIONS?*
copywriters/editors **clark malcolm, lois maasen**
printer **the etheridge company, grand rapids, michigan**
print run **60,000**
printing technique **six-color offset**
paper stock **warren lustro gloss**
design/prepress **computer** *(aldus pagemaker, aldus freehand, adobe photoshop)*
budget **$150,000**

64 *AIR HURACHE BROCHURE*
printer **diversified graphics**
print run **100,000**
printing technique **three-color process** *(vellum sheets),* **four-color process** *(coated paper),* **clear thermography, die-cut**
design/prepress **traditional and computer**
budget **$80,000**

This brochure explains the "Hurache" fit technology. It is round and the pages turn on a single grommet. The vellum sheets highlight specific features of the technology, and the photographs of the shoes reflect a futuristic attitude.

66 *FERTILITY & HORMONE CENTER BROCHURE*
production **steven newman**
printer **jds graphics, engelwood, new jersey**
print run **5,000**
design/prepress **computer** *(quark xpress, adobe photoshop)*

67 *AMES RESEARCH CENTER: THE FUTURE BEGNS HERE*

printer **starline printing inc., albuquerque, new mexico**

print run **10,000**

printing technique **four-color offset, spot varnish and additional special tinted flat varnish**

design/prepress **traditional**

budget **$97,000**

This 40-page multi-purpose brochure was used for recruiting and public affairs purposes.

68 *ENGELHARD CORPORATION 1992 ANNUAL REVIEW*

printer **philadelphia press, burlington, new jersey**

print run **60,000**

printing technique **four-color process, one match color and gloss varnish** *(cover and narrative),* **four-color process and one match color** *(insert),* **two match colors** *(financials)*

paper stock **luston gloss 100#** *(cover, text),* **gainsborough 80#** *(text)*

design/prepress **macintosh** *(quark xpress)*

72 *NIKE WOMEN'S DIVISION*

copywriter **mary mcmahn**

production manager **julia lambie**

printer **rono graphics**

print run **20,000**

paper stock **lustro dull**

design/prepress **macintosh** *(adobe illustrator)*

budget **$30,000**

To highlight Nike's market for women, this piece describes how different catagories are aligned within the women's marketing spectrum.

72 *TOPKOTE PAPER PROMOTION*

copywriter **christy brand**

printer **calsonic micira graphics, inc.**

print run **5,000**

printing technique **four-color process, two metallics and spot varnish**

paper stock **topkote**

design/prepress **macintosh quadra 950/800** *(quark xpress, adobe illustrator, adobe photoshop)*

budget **$35,000**

To promote Topkote Dull, each page of this brochure illustrated a different attribute of the paper.

75 *CONSOLIDATED CENTURA PLUS PROMOTION*

printer **lake county press, waukegan, illinois**

print run **80,000**

printing technique **four-color process and three match colors**

paper stock **consolidated centura plus 100#** *(cover, text)*

design/prepress **macintosh** *(quark xpress)*

This brochure was designed to be sent out individually or with another promotion, Centura Reflections II.

76 *TELEPORT COMMUNICATIONS BROCHURES*

production **steven newman**

printer **radiant graphics, new york, new york**

print run **3,000**

design/prepress **macintosh** *(quark xpress, adobe illustrator)*

77 *POTLATCH #5: NOT THE TIME TO COMPROMISE*

copywriter **craig frazier**

printer **watt peterson, minneapolis, minnesota**

print run **50,000**

printing technique **four-color process, one pms and varnish**

paper stock **potlatch vintage remarque**

design/prepress **macintosh** *(quark xpress, adobe photoshop)*

Images and words were used in this brochure to express a personal view of the subject of compromise.

78 *SPRINGHILL COATED COVER PROMOTION BROCHURE*

production manager **judy felker**

account manager **bill corkeet**

printer **b & m printing company, memphis, tennessee**

print run **40,000**

paper stock **springhill coated cover**

design/prepress **macintosh quadra 700** *(aldus freehand, adobe photoshop)*

budget **$90,000**

To promote a new blue-white shade of Springhill coated cover stock, this brochure compares the performance of the old shade versus the new.

79 *SAN ANTONIO: GET A FEEL FOR IT!*

printer **central life assurance, des moines, iowa**

print run **1,200**

printing technique **alternately screen printed on premium grade cover stock in silver and teal opaque inks, and offset printed on kraft paper in black ink** *(inside pages);* **visuals on the cover are varnished onto chipboard**

paper stock **james river tuscan 65# brick/brown** *(cover)*

design/prepress **traditional**

This brochure announced the annual meeting of the ICPA, an association of event and meeting planners. In keeping with the "San Antonio: Get a Feel for It" theme of the conference, this mailing included many textures and layers. A burlap bag was used for the envelope, and the brochure itself included leather and stamped metal.

82 *BLACK & DECKER 1991 ANNUAL REPORT*

printer **heritage press, dallas, texas**

print run **110,500**

printing technique **four-color process, five match colors and two varnishes** *(cover, text),* **two colors** *(financials)*

paper stock **parilux dull 92.5#** *(cover),* **parilux dull 100#** *(text),* **mohawk vellum 70# book**

design/prepress **traditional**

83 *SNAP-ON INC. 1992 ANNUAL REPORT*

printer **imperial lithographers, milwaukee, wisconsin**

print run **55,000**

printing technique **six-color, sheet-fed**

paper stock **consolidated**

design/prepress **computer** *(quark xpress)*

budget **$150,000**

84 *ADOBE SYSTEMS INC. 1992 ANNUAL REPORT*

printer **heritage press, dallas, texas**

paper stock **consolidated futura matte recycled**

design/prepress **macintosh** *(post script software)*

To position Adobe as a company that stands for communication software and creative expression, software demonstrations and commercial samples created with Adobe software were used. Among these examples were an Absolute Vodka ad created with Adobe Photoshop and a series of frames for a U2 music video created with Adobe Premiere.

85 *LASERTECHNICS INC. 1993 ANNUAL REPORT*

printer **chapagne printing, houston, texas**

print run **8,000**

paper stock **champion benefit 80# celery** *(cover),* **champion benefit 70# ochre** *(text),* **champion benefit 70# chalk** *(text),* **potlach karma 80# white** *(text)*

design/prepress **macintosh centris 650** *(quark xpress)*

The division of one company into two was visually represented by perforations and die cuts, while keeping the simple look of 1992's annual report.

86 *PAST IS PRESENT BROCHURE*

production **steven newman**

printer **jds graphics, englewood, new jersey**

print run **3,000**

design/prepress **macintosh** *(quark xpress, adobe photoshop)*

88 *BRØDERBUND SOFTWARE 1992 ANNUAL REPORT*

printer **graphic center, sacramento, california**

print run **75,000**

printing technique **four-color process and matte/gloss varnish, die-cut cover**

paper stock **starwhite vicksburg 80# tierra, vintage velvet 100# gloss**

design/prepress **traditional and macintosh** *(quark xpress)*

budget **$105,000**

For their first annual report, Brøderbund wanted an interactive book to highlight their software products. Visual product icons in the table of contents take the reader through the book, while reflecting the interactive nature of the company's products. Actual screen capture images were used instead of photography, resulting in significant savings.

89 *RASETEROPS 1993 ANNUAL REPORT*

printer **graphic arts center, portland, oregon**

print run **20,000**

printing technique **four-color process, one match color and varnish**

paper stock **reflections esse**

design/prepress **macintosh centra 650** *(quark xpress)*

budget **$100,000**

The theme of this annual report was "Keeping the Competitive Edge." RasterOps customer stories highlight the areas where RasterOps products are being used, and computer graphics show the capabilities of RasterOps boards and monitors.

90 *AMERICAN CANCER SOCIETY 1992 ANNUAL REPORT*

printer **color graphics, atlanta, georgia**

print run **3,000**

printing technique **2/2**

paper stock **simpson evergreen, simpson sundance felt**

design/prepress **computer** *(quark xpress)*

budget **$5,000** *(design and art pro-bono)*

A dollar across the bottom of the foldout shows how the money is spent, while text discusses the charity in more detail.

91 *COMSAT CORPORATION 1992 ANNUAL REPORT*

printer **acme printing company, wilmington, massachusetts**

print run **90,000**

paper stock **warren recovery gloss cover 100#** *(cover, text),* **crosspointe medallion white** *(text)*

92 *MARCAM CORPORATION 1992 ANNUAL REPORT*

printer **allied printing, manchester, connecticut**

print run **15,000**

printing technique **six-color, two offline varnishes** *(dull, tinted dull),* **halftones printed over flat match colors**

paper stock **potlatch vintage, curtis brightwater**

design/prepress **traditional and macintosh** *(quark xpress, aldus freehand)*

budget **$60,000**

A series of four customer case studies with testamonials, facts, and figures illustrates the bottom-line benefits of Marcam's application solutions for the process industries.

93 METROPOLITAN LIFE 1993 ANNUAL REPORT

printer **george rice & sons, los angeles, california**

print run **85,000**

printing technique **thermography** (cover)

paper stock **simpson equinox summer 80# white** (cover), **simpson equinox autumn 80# blush** (text), **zanders ikonofi 100# matte** (text)

design/prepress **macintosh** (quark xpress)

A series of large and inviting black-and-white photographs of families at various stages of life are accompanied by colorful type reading "Metlife at 30…40…50…60" and flanked by Peanuts-style icons that illustrate Metlife products and services relevant to a family at each stage.

94 THE MEAD CORPORATION 1993 ANNUAL REPORT

account executive **barbara weisen**

supervisor **leslie segal**

printer **the hennegan company**

print run **90,000**

printing technique **four-color process**

paper stock **signature gloss 100#** (cover), **gilbert esse texture 80# accent yellow** (flyleaf), **signature gloss 100#** (text), **gilbert esse 80# light gray/green/red/light gray blue** (text)

design/prepress **macintosh**

This annual report presented examples of how the company is achieving its objectives in terms of customer satisfaction, productivity, and high performance and management.

95 BLACK & DECKER 1992 ANNUAL REPORT

printer **heritage press, dallas, texas**

print run **120,000**

printing technique **five match colors and varnish over two match colors and varnish** (cover), **six colors and offline varnish** (text), **five colors** (short pages), **two colors** (financials)

paper stock **quintessence remarque gloss 100#** (cover, text), **mohawk dove 70# gray** (text), **monadnock revue 80#** (text)

design/prepress **macintosh** (quark xpress)

96 OMI CORP. 1993 ANNUAL REPORT

printer **acme printing company, wilmington, massachusetts**

print run **20,000**

printing technique **5/4** (cover), **7/7** (narrative), **2/2** (financials)

paper stock **warren lustro** (cover, text), **crosspointe passport smooth gypsum** (text)

design/prepress **macintosh quadra 840** (adobe illustrator)

The cover utilizes a red touch plate in the four-color subject.

97 THE NEIMAN MARCUS GROUP 1993 ANNUAL REPORT

printer **hennegan, cincinnati, ohio**

print run **32,000**

printing technique **four-color process, one match color and varnish**

paper stock **zanders konorex 100#, hopper proterra alabaster gill clear**

design/prepress **macintosh quadra 700** (quark xpress)

Highly stylized black-and-white photography shows the unique characteristics of each company.

98 NIKE INC. 1992 ANNUAL REPORT

copywriter **bob lambie**

printer **irwin hodson, portland, oregon**

print run **110,000**

paper stock **iconolux, speckletone**

design/prepress **traditional**

This annual report was designed to celebrate 20 years of innovation in sports and fitness. Nine spreads focus on different areas of the company. A lot of excitement was created through the use of unpredictable and innovative imagery.

99 EXPEDITORS INTERNATIONAL 1992 ANNUAL REPORT

printer **h. macdonald printing, richmond, canada**

print run **10,000**

printing technique **six match colors, offset, hand-tipped cover plate**

paper stock **gainsborough vintage/starwhite**

design/prepress **macintosh quadra** (aldus pagemaker, aldus freehand)

budget **$75,000**

The illustrations used were derived from specific company statistics.

100 LASERTECHNICS 1992 ANNUAL REPORT

computer production **nathan james**

printer **prisma graphic, phoenix, arizona**

print run **10,000**

paper stock **french durotone packing carton 145#** (cover), **french speckletone kraft 80#** (cover), **simpson lamonite safety paper basketweave gray**

design/prepress **macintosh iici** (quark xpress)

Since the company had lost money, they wanted the annual report to be the opposite of the flashy reports of years past and show a new direction. To accomplish this, no photographs were used, only type and interesting paper.

101 PHOENIX RE CORPORATION 1992 ANNUAL REPORT

printer **franklin graphics, nashville, tennessee**

print run **5,000**

printing technique **four-color process and dull/gloss varnish**

paper stock **simpson evergreen, diamoute gloss**

design/prepress **computer** (quark xpress)

budget **$30-35,000**

102 SAN FRANCISCO AIRPORT COMMISSION 1993 ANNUAL REPORT

printer **fong & fong, sacramento, california**

printing technique **four-color process**

paper stock **simpson gainsborough 88# cover plus ebony** (cover), **champion benefit 80# cover, flintstone white** (text)

design/prepress **macintosh** (quark xpress, adobe illustrator)

The theme of this annual report was the economic impact of the San Francisco International Airport on the Bay Area. In each chapter, the key financial or quantitative figure was emphasized in order to show its importance. This was combined with a photographic visual that both illustrates the number and relates to the subject of the chapter.

103 HERMAN MILLER 1993 ANNUAL REPORT

copywriter/editor **clark malcolm**

typesetters **rita endres, kim lapp**

production manager **marlene capotosto**

printer **burch, inc., benton harbor, michigan**

print run **25,000**

printing technique **offset, embossing, glued tip-ons, film lamination**

paper stock **champion carnival 90# opaque** (cover), **champion carnival 70#/80# smooth/vellum, eloquence gloss 110#, u.v. ultra ii 17# radiant white, ardor bond 16#, neenah environment bond 24# natural, champion mystique laid 70# bright white, springhill offset 60# canary, french durotone 60# butcher off-white**

design/prepress **computer** (quark xpress, aldus freehand, adobe photoshop)

budget **$200,000**

---

104 ADVO INC. ANNUAL REPORT

printer **donald blyler offset, lebanon, pennsylvania**

printing technique **four-color process and two match colors, offset**

paper stock **potlatch vintage gloss**

design/prepress **macintosh** (quark xpress, adobe illustrator, adobe photoshop)

105 TAMBRANDS 1993 ANNUAL REPORT

printer **george rice & sons, new york, new york**

print run **30,000**

printing technique **five-color and varnish**

paper stock **simpson kashmir**

design/prepress **macintosh**

This annual report focuses on Tambrands strengths and strategies for growth, with their strategies symbolized by photographic highlights of the human body that link to various aspects of communication. The images are soft in color and focus, yet when combined with large typography, the message is strong and clear.

106 UNITED WATER RESOURCES 1993 ANNUAL REPORT

printer **acme printing company, wilmington, massachusetts**

print run **50,000**

printing technique **four-color process and two pms with a clear foil** (cover), **6/6 and 2/2** (text)

paper stock **simpson evergreen** (cover), **warren lustro** (text), **james river graphika vellum** (text)

design/prepress **traditional and macintosh quadra 840** (quark xpress, aldus freehand, adobe illustrator)

107 TOSCO CORPORATION 1993 ANNUAL REPORT

printer **daniels printing company, everett, massachusetts**

print run **52,000**

printing technique **5/4, diecut** (cover), **6/6** (text), **2/2** (narrative)

paper stock **warren lustro recycled** (cover, text), **james river graphika lineal**

design/prepress **traditional and macintosh quadra 840** (adobe illustrator)

108 THE PROGRESSIVE CORPORATION 1992 ANNUAL REPORT

copywriter **peter b. lewis**

art curator **toby d. lewis**

printer **fortran printing, inc.**

print run **32,000**

printing technique **four-color process, three match colors, gloss and dull varnish** (cover), **four-color process and two match colors** (coated), **five match colors and black**

paper stock **potlatch quintessence remarque 100# velvet cover/coated** (cover, text), **strathmore renewal uncoated 80# white** (text)

design/prepress **macintosh quadra** (quark xpress)

To highlight the importance of teamwork, employees were invited to nominate a collegue whom they felt had made a contribution to Progressive's success. The photographer's composite biographical puzzles provide insight into each person's uniqueness through the juxtaposition of personal possessions with quotations about each person from teammates.

109 THF PROMUS COMPANIES 1993 ANNUAL REPORT

printer **acme printing company, wilmington, massachusetts**

print run **99,000**

printing technique **6 + emboss/4** (cover), **7/7** (text)

paper stock **zanders ikonofix recycled gloss** (cover, text)

design/prepress **macintosh centris 660, quadra 840** (quark xpress, adobe illustrator, adobe photoshop)

110 KETCH *1992 ANNUAL REPORT*
printer **donlevy lithograph, inc., wichita, kansas**
budget **$20,000**

This piece was a combination annual report and three-year plan for KETCH. The intent was to draw the reader into the text with a series of futurist illustrations, each demonstrating a specific section of the plan. As this plan was to serve for three years, the financials were printed as a foldout which attached only the first year's reports.

111 GEORGIA-PACIFIC CORPORATION *1993 ANNUAL REPORT*
production manager **susan mechnig**
computer production **jack jacobi**
retouching **dan kraemer**
printer **george rice & sons, los angeles, california**
print run **250,000**
printing technique **six-color process, sheet fed** *(cover),* **six-color process, web** *(body)*
paper stock **hopper® proterra™ flecks™ chalk 100#** *(cover),* **hopper® proterra™ flecks™ chalk 70#** *(text)*
design/prepress **traditional**

The narrative was segmented into four reports, each visually tied to different operations forrest areas.

112 KNOWLEDGEWARE *1993 ANNUAL REPORT*
printer **harris specialty lithographix, stone mountain, georgia**
print run **50,000**
printing technique **six-color with aqueous coating**
paper stock **zanders ikonotix gloss champion benefit**
design/prepress **macintosh** *(quark xpress, adobe illustrator)*

114 AMERICA ONLINE INC. *1993 ANNUAL REPORT*
printer **daniels printing company, everett, massachusetts**
print run **20,000**
printing technique **four-color process and three pms colors**
paper stock **reflections gloss 100#** *(cover, text)*
design/prepress **traditional and macintosh** *(quark xpress, adobe illustrator, adobe photoshop)*
budget **$67,000 plus printing**

115 COMSAT CORPORATION *1993 ANNUAL REPORT*
printer **acme printing company, wilmington, massachusetts**
print run **90,000**
printing technique **7/4** *(cover),* **6/6** *(narrative),* **4/4 and 2/2** *(financials)*
paper stock **warren recovery** *(cover, text),* **bellbrook laid**
design/prepress **traditional and macintosh quadra 840** *(adobe illustrator)*

116 HORIZON HEALTHCARE CORPORATION *QUARTERLIES AND ANNUAL REPORT*
printer **l & m printing, denver, colorado**
print run **5,700** *(quarterlies),* **11,000** *(annual reports)*
paper stock **simpson starwhite vicksburg 80#** *(cover),* **potlatch karma 80# white** *(text)*
design/prepress **macintosh iicx** *(quark xpress, aldus freehand, adobe photoshop)*

Images of a rose in bloom were used in these pieces to show growth.

117 DURACELL *1992 ANNUAL REPORT*
copywriters **michael clive, jim donahue**
printer **heritage press, dallas, texas**
print run **40,000**
paper stock **french paper company speckletone 80# black, mead paper signature dull 80#, strathmore paper renewal 80# moss**
design/prepress **macintosh** *(quark xpress, adobe photoshop)*

To demonstrate the strength and growth potential of Duracell, the copy and photos "grow" as the reader progresses through the annual report.

118 KING WORLD PRODUCTIONS *1993 ANNUAL REPORT*
printer **innovation printing, philadelphia, pennsylvania**
print run **20,000**
printing technique **offset**
paper stock **recollections matte coated 80#/100#** *(cover, text)*
design/prepress **traditional and macintosh**

This annual report showcases King World's award-winning programs while providing a special report on Inside Edition in a small booklet that can be removed.

119 WESTERN WATER *1993 ANNUAL REPORT*
printer **pace lithographers, city of industry, california**
print run **7,500**
paper stock **reflections gloss 100#** *(cover, text)*
design/prepress **traditional and macintosh iici** *(quark xpress)*
budget **$22,000 plus printing**

To produce an eye-catching annual report, the designers used well-illustrated graphs and charts, and full-color stock photography.

120 CLUB MED, INC. *1993 ANNUAL REPORT*
printer **acme printing company, wilmington, massachusetts**
print run **11,000**
printing technique **four pms, black and varnish** *(cover),* **6/6** *(text),* **2/2** *(financials)*
paper stock **simpson sundance felt** *(cover, text),* **warren lustro gloss** *(text)*
design/prepress **traditional and macintosh quadra 840** *(adobe illustrator)*

121 REEBOK INTERNATIONAL *1990 ANNUAL REPORT*
supervisor **leslie segal**
project manager **barbara weisen**
printer **acme printing company, wilmington, massachusetts**
print run **100,000**
printing technique **offset**
paper stock **lustro gloss/dull** *(cover, text)*

To dramatically show Reebok's historical involvement in the Olympics, this annual report incorporates a foldout poster about the Olympics featuring an athlete wearing only Reeboks.

122 US WEST FOUNDATION *1990–1991 ANNUAL REVIEW*
printer **diversified graphics, minneapolis, minnesota**
print run **20,000**
paper stock **potlatch quintessence remarque 100# velvet** *(cover),* **cross pointe genesis 80# milkweed** *(text),* **simpson quest moss 80#** *(text)*
design/prepress **traditional**

This annual report shows how funds were spent both verbally and graphically.

123 PRESBYTERIAN HEALTHCARE *1992 ANNUAL REPORT*
printer **l & m printing, denver, colorado**
print run **4,000**
paper stock **simpson evergreen 80# kraft** *(cover),* **potlatch karma dull 65# white** *(cover),* **simpson evergreen 70# oak** *(text)*
design/prepress **traditional**

Sympathetic images were used to help raise money, and the wire-o binding encourages donors to keep the book.

124 TIME WARNER *1991 ANNUAL REPORT*
copywriter **time warner**
typography **fbp & pastore, de pamphilis, rampone, and royal** *(financials)*
printer **l. p. thebault company, parsippany, new jersey**
print run **280,000** *(english),* **5,000** *(german, french, italian, spanish),* **10,000** *(japanese)*
printing technique **four-color process and two pms**
paper stock **gilbert paper esse custom duplex textured 80# white/dark grey blue, gilbert paper esse smooth/textured 70# white/yellow**
design/prepress **macintosh** *(quark xpress, adobe photoshop)*

126 THE BISYS GROUP *1993 ANNUAL REPORT*
printer **toppan printing company, inc., somerset, new jersey**
print run **15,000**
printing technique **four-color process and one pms on pages with text, liquid lamination** *(covers)*
paper stock **quintessence remarque gloss 100#** *(text, cover)*
design/prepress **macintosh ii cx** *(quark xpress, adobe illustrator)*
budget **$90,000**

The testimonials and photography used throughout this annual report show solutions which improve the profitability, performance, and competitive position of all types of financial organizations in a very abstract way.

127 E.I. DU PONT DE NEMOURS *1992 ANNUAL REPORT*
copywriters **justin carisio, maury bates**
print run **550,000**
printing technique **four-color process and pms overall gloss varnish, 1-2-4c and pms overall gloss varnish two sides**
paper stock **s.d. warren recovery matte 70#, s.d. warren futura matte 70# white, manistique 46# tablet white**
design/prepress **computer**

129 L G & E ENERGY CORP. *1993 ANNUAL REPORT*
printer **bradley, des plaines, illinois**
print run **100,000**
printing technique **6/6, die-cut cover, spot gloss varnish**
paper stock **ikonofix matte, hopper proterra flecks**
design/prepress **computer** *(quark xpress)*

133 NEW YORK TELEPHONE PROMOTIONAL MAILER
production **steven newman**
printer **candid litho**
design/prepress **macintosh** *(quark xpress)*

134 MOHAWK PAPER MILLS
printing technique **two match colors and inline spot varnish** *(dust jacket),* **two hits matte black, one match color, inline overall matte varnish** *(p. 1-12),* **four-color process, one match color, inline aqueous coating** *(p. 13-23),* **four-color process** *(p. 24-31, 65-75),* **duotones, match gray solid, inline spot tinted matte varnish** *(p. 32-40),* **four-color process and two match colors** *(41-48),* **two hits matte black, one match color, inline spot matte varnish** *(p. 49-57),* **black and four match colors** *(58-64),* **black and one match color** *(76-80),* **sheetfed on a six-unit heidelberg using 175 line screen**
paper stock **mohawk vellum text 70# gold** *(dust jacket),* **mohawk satin 65# charcoal** *(cover),* **mohawk superfine smooth 80# white** *(text),* **mohawk 50/10 gloss/matte 100#/80#** *(text),* **mohawk p/c 100 80#** *(text),* **mohawk chlorfree gloss 100#** *(text)*
design/prepress
macintosh *(quark xpress)*

SIMPSON NEO: INOVATION AND REDISCOVERY
printer **heritage press, dallas, texas**
print run **60,000**
printing technique **offset**
paper stock **coronado sst recycled, equinox sunrise gold, sundance navajo white, evergreen web gloss, quest putty, evergreen birch cord, evergreen matte natural, equinox spring mist**
design/prepress **traditional and computer**

This piece incorporated several coated and uncoated Simpson products, with an emphasis on recycled products. To reflect the theme "Innovation with Traditional Ideas," a new, magazine-style format was used.

137 **MIRA WEB/MIRA GLOSS PAPER PROMOTION**
printer **case-hoyt**
print run **30,000**
printing technique **web offset**
paper stock **spring hill mira web/gloss**
design/prepress **macintosh** *(quark xpress)*

138 **O WHAT A RELEAF**
copywriter **wendy lyons**
printer **madison press, madison, wisconsin**
print run **50,000**
printing technique **offset**
paper stock **howard paper crushed leaf**
design/prepress **traditional**

To demonstrate the advantages of using Crushed Leaf paper, this paper promotion utilized several effects, including halftones, line art, and metallic inks.

140 **ELSEWARE FOLDER**
printer **george rice & sons, seattle, washington**
print run **2,000**
printing technique **7 pms/2 pms with gloss varnish seal**
paper stock **classic crest 80# solar white** *(cover)*
design/prepress **macintosh iici** *(aldus freehand)*

To emphasize the client's focus on typography as an art form, large type used as imagery was combined with quotes about type from noted designers.

141 **AGI DIGIPAK TIMES TWO**
printer **carqueville/tcr graphics, streamwood, illinois**
print run **5,000**
printing technique **silkscreen** *(cover),* **four-color process** *(coated pages),* **two colors** *(uncoated pages)*
paper stock **wynstone supermatch kraft 130#** *(cover),* **wynstone brown kraft** *(body)*
design/prepress **computer** *(aldus freehand)*

This brochure was used as a promotional handout at a recording industry trade show. It mimics the CD format using the client's products, since AGI provides CD packaging to the recording industry.

142 **TUNE INTO WRGC**
copywriter **sheree clark**
printer **acme printing, des moines, iowa**
print run **2,000**
printing technique **two match colors, offset**
paper stock **james river graphika**
design/prepress **traditional**

This program emphasizes the radio theme of the Western Regional Greek Conference with radio, music, and sound graphics executed throughout in red, black, and white.

143 **MOORE LABELS GETS STUCK ON GREAT IDEAS BROCHURE**
printer **abell, pearson printing, wichita, kansas**
print run **3,000**
printing technique **die cutting, embossing, offset lithography, nine-color litho labels, short sheets and spiral binding**
paper stock **french paper speckletone**
design/prepress **traditional and macintosh** *(quark xpress)*
budget **$10,000**

This was designed as an interactive brochure; the recipient actually removes and applies labels. By giving customers a chance to play with Moore label products first-hand, the quality of the product is demonstrated in a fun way.

144 **HAYMARKET SQUARE BROCHURE**
printer **edwards graphic arts, des moines, iowa**
print run **2,000**
printing technique **six pms, black foil, die-cut, wire-o binding**
paper stock **kromekote**
design/prepress **macintosh** *(quark xpress, aldus freehand)*
budget **$10,000**

This piece uses bold graphics in a humorous way to market a shopping mall.

145 **ENVIRONMENT PAPER CAMPAIGN**
production manager **robin salter**
account executive **chris martin**
printer **castle-pierce, fey publishing, myers printing company**
print run **40,000**
printing technique **separate run of black for photos**
paper stock **neenah environment**
design/prepress **macintosh** *(quark xpress)*

To set Neenah's recycled line of uncoated paper apart from competitors and appeal to the Generation X mindset, an "In Your Face" image was created rather than using imagery of birds, flowers, and trees.

146 **SEPARATING COLOR PHOTOGRAPHY**
printer **l.p. thebault, parsippany, new jersey**
printing technique **four-color process with substitutions including fluorescent yellow and magenta, magenta touch plate**
paper stock **monadnock astrolite 80#/65#** *(cover)*
design/prepress **macintosh quadra 900** *(adobe photoshop)*

The second in a series of technical brochures, this piece explores critical areas of the prepress process and how each can be applied to achieve the best end results. The cover image was used as a positive image, and then this same image was inverted and solarized for the inside covers.

147 **MOHAWK 50/10 PAPER PROMOTION**
printer **burch incorporated**
print run **40,000**
printing technique **sheetfed**
paper stock **mohawk 50/10**
design/prepress **macintosh** *(quark xpress)*

148 **NEOTONE-2**
printer **daniels printing company, everett, massachusetts**
printing technique **200 line four-color and one match color using soy-based inks**
paper stock **monadnock astrolite 80#** *(cover),* **monadnock astrolite 100#** *(text)*
design/prepress **macintosh** *(quark xpress)*

This piece explores new options in darkroom techniques and digital manipulation that enhance or alter the mood of an image, including tonal layering, cross-processing, electronic coloring/layering, and reverse/subtractive coloring.

149 **VITRA OVERVIEW 1993**
chairman **ralph fehlbaum**
marketing communications **judith brauner**
printing technique **offset**
design/prepress **macintosh**
budget **$31,500**

The designers' objective was to create a simple, sympathetic media that gives an overview of all products, states references, and includes the advertising campaign (personalities).

150 **ONE BY ONE**
copywriter **wendy lyons**
printer **artcraft, des moines, iowa**
print run **26,000**
printing technique **offset using only black ink, puzzle and box were laminated to chipboard, die-cut**
paper stock **gilbert oxford**
design/prepress **traditional**

The client wanted to demonstrate the creative possibilities afforded by one color of ink—one color, one designer. By using screens of black and several paper stocks, the designer was able to create the illusion of more than one color in the project. The jigsaw puzzle beneath the brochure was an added bonus.

152 **ARLINGTON NATIONAL RACECOURT PROMOTIONAL BROCHURE**
copywriter **gary gusick**
printer **universal lithographers inc., sheboygan, wisconsin**
print run **20,000**
printing technique **four-color process and overall varnish**
paper stock **consolidated reflections**
design/prepress **traditional and computer** *(aldus freehand)*

This sellable momento communicates various facts about how a thoroughbred racetrack functions. The nonlinear design emphasizes the short focus of attention, perhaps between races. Betting, wagering, and other important functions are prominently highlighted while other less important, yet interesting bits of information are hidden in the flaps. The pastel illustrations were scanned directly from original art.

154 **"IN'S" OF IMAGE LETTERHEAD KIT**
printer **bogart's printing, erie, pennsylvania**
print run **45,000**
printing technique **thermography, die-cut, embossing**
paper stock **classic linen, classic laid, classic crest, uv ultra**
design/prepress **traditional and macintosh** *(quark xpress)*

This kit, presented as a gift, contained letterhead samples on premium uncoated paper. Visually and editorially, the package educates the audience on trends in image and identity design and printing techniques.

155 **ADVANTAGE POINT**
printer **macdonald & evans, inc., braintree, massachusetts**
print run **5,000**
printing technique **touchplates on the process color, spot matte and gloss varnishes**
paper stock **reflections gloss 85#** *(cover, text),* **concrete text 80#** *(interleaves)*
design/prepress **macintosh**
budget **$50,000**

156 GALLERY MONTHLY MAGAZINE
printer **vip printing, mordialloc, australia**
print run **15,000**
printing technique **lithographic offset**
design/prepress **macintosh** (quark xpress)
budget **$8,000-10,000**

To reflect quality and an appreciation of fine art, the designers used Bernhard Modern for the masthead, captions and title sections of this magazine.

157 "SHOW QUALITY" CENTURA PROMOTION
printer **lake county press, waukegan, illinois**
printing technique **four-color process, special colors, spot varnish and metallic inks**
paper stock **centura gloss 100#** (cover, text)
design/prepress **traditional and macintosh**

158 EP/CSAD CATALOG
produciton manager **robin salter**
printer **i p d printing**
print run **40,000**
design/prepress **macintosh** (quark xpress, adobe photoshop)

159 DU PONT PRESSKIT
production **steven newman**
printer **radiant graphics, new york, new york**
print run **2,500**
design/prepress **macintosh** (quark xpress, adobe illustrator)

160 LETTER PERFECT® FINE PAPERS LETTER FOLDER
printer **bogart's graphics group, erie, pennsylvania**
printing technique **eight-color process with clear thermography** (outside), **five-color process** (inside)
paper stock **classic® linen 100# avon brilliant white** (cover), **u/v ultra® ii translucent printing paper 171#** (outside wrap), **classic® linen, classic® lzid, classic crest writing 24#**
design/prepress **macintosh quadra 700** (adobe illustrator)

To market new colors of Neenah Paper's three premium writing sheets, the same six letterhead designs were used across three different finishes of the papers.

162 CIB SALES KIT
printer **burmeister lithography, new york, new york**
print run **3,500**
budget **$9,500**

To market an illustration directory, a direct mailer was followed by this sales kit which mirrored the design of the illustration directory. Interviews with clients and art directors who used the book reinforced its value.

163 GRAPHIC ARTS CENTER "IMAGE" BROCHURE
printer **graphic arts center, portland, oregon**
print run **15,000**
printing technique **four-color process with metallic inks in two passes on 640** (text), **three-color process, two sides using pastel inks** (fly sheets), **four-color, one pms and black** (label)
paper stock **supermatch kraft 130# natural** (cover), **eloquence gloss 110# white** (text), **debonair gloss label 60# white** (labels), **cottonwood vellum 70# evergreen** (flysheets)
design/prepress **traditional**
budget **$200,000**

164 BRADLEY WEB PROMOTION "YES NO"
printer **bradley printing company**
print run **80,000**
printing technique **web, offset**
paper stock **consolidated paper reflections gloss web 90#** (text), **strathmore grandee 80#** (cover)
design/prepress **macintosh** (quark xpress)
budget **$55,000**

This Z-fold book compares Bradley's web printing with sheetfed printing to show that the end results are equal.

165 COMPATIBLEENVIRONMENTS
printer **neenah printing, neenah, wisconsin**
printing technique **lithography, three-color process** (outside), **four-color process** (inside), **scoring, die-cut**
paper stock **environment® wave finish 80# natural white** (folder)
design/prepress **traditional**

To promote the use of recycled paper in both the business and creative communities, a clean European style was combined with artistic imagery. A recycled pencil was used to connect the folder which contained 11 samples of Environment® Writing letterheads.

168 NEC CD-ROM
printer **george rice & sons, los angeles, california**
print run **75,000**
printing technique **six-color process, offset**
paper stock **westvaco celesta**
design/prepress **macintosh** (quark xpress, adobe illustrator, adobe photoshop)

169 NOIE ET BLANC
printer **burch inc., michigan**
print run **80,000**
printing technique **sheetfed**
paper stock **potlatch quintessence**
design/prepress **macintosh** (quark xpress)

170 NATIONAL TRAVELERS LIFE 85TH ANNIVERSARY
copywriter **wendy lyons**
printers **acme printing company, wilmington, massachusetts; national travelers life, des moines, iowa**
print run **1,200**
printing technique **four-color process and two match colors, offset**
paper stock **james river terra cote/tuscan terra**
design/prepress **traditional**

This brochure, developed to commemorate the company's 85th anniversary and promote a sales incentive trip to the Caribbean, was mailed in a custom-designed box with coordinating slip-band.

171 1992 CALENDAR
printer **lithographix, los angeles, california**
print run **5,000**
printing technique **6/0**
paper stock **reflections tapestry** (case), **parchtone vellum** (wrap)
design/prepress **traditional and computer**
budget **$80,000**

To promote Lithographix and Butler Paper, 12 designers collaborated with the printer and paper company to create this calendar.

172 LUMIÉRE
printer **baker gurney & mclarten press ltd.**
print run **20,000**
printing technique **photographic images direct from lumiére system, folders lithographed with two blacks, plus two offline varnishes—two sides**
paper stock **10 point, cachet cover, gloss white**

To demonstrate the possibilities of Lumiére, three electronic images and a namestyle were created. Promotional folders were developed which allowed actual Lumiére proofs to be inserted and later updated for customized presentations.

176 THE EDUCATION DIVISION 1993-1994 CATALOG
production **steven newman**
paper stock **evergreen uv**
design/prepress **macintosh iici** (quark xpress)

This catalog focuses on children and the abilities arts foster. Six abilities are highlighted—skill, creativity, self-esteem, understanding, values, and goals. At the beginning of each section one of the words and its definition is printed on a half sheet of vellum. This half page is followed by a quote from either an educator or child about how the arts have enhanced their lives along with a fun photograph of a child's face.

178 WRGC 45TH ANNIVERSARY MATERIALS
printer **artcraft, des moines, iowa**
print run **1,800**
printing technique **two match colors, offset**
design/prepress **traditional**

A 4" x 5" brochure featuring interesting typography and graphic illustrations was developed to promote conference registration. Coordinating materials (notebooks, posters, and awards) completed the campaign.

179 CLEVELAND INSTITUTE OF ART 1993-1994 CATALOG
copywriter **anne brooks ranallo**
printer **fortran printing, inc.**
print run **48,000**
printing technique **four-color process, match red and gloss varnish** (covers, interior pages), **two white, black, match red, and gloss varnish** (flysheet)
paper stock **s.d. warren lustro dull recycled 100#/80#** (cover, text), **gilbert gilclear medium vellum** (fly sheet)
printing technique **200 line four-color process**
design/prepress **traditional and macintosh** (quark xpress, adobe photoshop)

180 ALL STAR CO-OP BOOK
copywriter **rich swietek**

181 PREVENTIVE HEALTH CARE MAILER
printer **color graphics**
print run **30,000**
printing technique **four match colors, lithography**
paper stock **starwhite vicksburg**
design/prepress **traditional and macintosh iici** (quark xpress, adobe illustrator)
budget **$28,000 plus printing**

Southern California Edison was initiating a series of health risk tests for employees and needed an easy-to-understand direct mail package that contained an incentive. "The No Sweat Rebate Program" theme emphasized that the program would require little or no effort. A rebate pass was included in the colorful and reader-friendly package.

182 THE PENCIL. SIMPLE IN FORM. POWERFUL IN FUNCTION.
copywriter **mary mcdonald lewis**
printer **color litho, los angeles, california**
print run **6,000**
paper stock **potlatch northwest gloss 80#/100#** (cover), **james river curtis parchment parchkin 50# fibra**
design/prepress **macintosh iici** (quark xpress, adobe photoshop)
budget **all services pro bono**

This self-promotional piece was to be unique, thought provoking, graphically exciting and a showcase for the talent and services of those involved.

233

184 PHILIP MORRIS IS COMMITTED TO YOUR SUCCESS
production **steven newman**
design/prepress **macintosh quadra 800**
(quark xpress, adobe illustrator)

185 DETAILS: ORDER NOW CATALOG
printer **meehan tooker, east rutherford, new jersey**
print run **30,000**
paper stock **gilbert esse**
design/prepress **macintosh** *(quark xpress, adobe illustrator, aldus freehand)*

The purpose of this piece was to position Details as concerned and knowledgeable about the health of a workplace. The information was divided into hierarchies, with problems/solutions first, and then a descending order of information from general to specific in separate sections.

186 GREENLEAF MEDICAL CORPORATE LITERATURE SERIES
copywriter **morgan thomas**
printer **ar lithographers, hayward, california**
print run **10,000**
printing technique **four-color process and spot gloss varnish, offset**
paper stock **simpson sequoia matte 65#** *(cover)*
design/prepress **traditional and macintosh iici** *(quark xpress, adobe illustrator)*
budget **$8,000** *(design),* **$16,000** *(printing)*

Multi-layered photo collages and a modular organization of information were used to convey the depth and versatility of a new computerized evaluation system for hand surgeons and therapists.

187 SUBJECTIVE REASONING
copywriter **peter watrous**
printer **lebanon valley offset, inc.**
printing technique **200 line, six colors, three passes, offset**
paper stock **kromekote recycled 25#** *(cover)*
design/prepress **macintosh quadra 800** *(quark xpress)*

This paper promotion was part of a series conceived by Drenttel Doyle Partners with Pentagram.

188 ANARA HOLISTIC HEALTH SPA IDENTITY COLLATERAL
printer **bradley printing company, des plaines, illinois**
print run **80,000**
paper stock **classic crest reflections**
design/prepress **traditional**
budget **$200,000**

To generate interest in the hotel's spa about to be opened, these pieces created the exotic, sensual feel of the spa's philosophy and the surrounding environment of Hawaii.

190 CORNING INC. EMPLOYEE BENEFITS HANDBOOK
printer **canfield & tack inc., rochester, new york; bok industries, leroy, new york** *(cloth binder)*
print run **18,000**
printing technique **two-color cloth wrap with six-color tip-in label** *(binder),* **two-color, short-cut omega-bound cover** *(overview brochure)*
paper stock **champion benefits natural flax 80#/70#** *(cover, text)*
design/prepress **traditional and computer** *(aldus pagemaker)*
budget **$250,000**

The strategy for this employee benefits handbook was to communicate prudent spending and substantial value, and to present the material in an organized and easy-to-understand format that was also friendly and personal. The use of uncoated recycled paper provided a lower cost appearance, and the paper characteristics were warm, soft and tactile.

191 1994 TROXEL PRODUCT BROCHURE
printer **o'neil printing, phoenix, arizona**
print run **35,000**
printing technique **four-color process, black tinted spot varnish** *(covers)*
paper stock **beckett expressions 80# text**
design/prepress **macintosh** *(quark xpress, adobe photoshop)*
budget **$35,000**

Location photography captured the subject matter that accurately defined each target audience. Studio photography, supported by the copy, conveyed the advanced technical design of each helmet.

192 LUNAR DESIGN CORPORATE IDENTITY MATERIALS
printer **techni-graphics, san francisco, california**
print run **1,000** *(presentation folders)*
design/prepress **macintosh**

The new Lunar corporate identity system is distinctive, and its classic graphic tone avoids trendiness. In an effort to communicate Lunar's approach to design and potential clients, multi-image sheets were designed to focus on human interaction with the product. These modular, computer-generated sheets can be updated to show new pieces from Lunar's portfolio.

194 ANNIEGLASS: ART COMES TO THE TABLE
printer **color copy printing, redwood city, california**
print run **5,000**
printing technique **offset, foil-stamping, copper wire-o binding**
paper stock **chipboard, starwhite vicksburg, kromekote 2000**
design/prepress **traditional**
budget **$30,000**

Beautifully composed photography was used to create a sales catalog that would reflect the handmade beauty and richness of Annieglass glassware. The unusual mix of printing, foil-stamping, die-cutting, binding and typography create an exciting display of textures, shapes, and colors.

195 MTV MEDIA KIT
copywriter **danny abelson**
printer **tanagraphics**
printing technique **six-color, sheetfed, wire-o binding**
paper stock **heavy weight kroyden flex** *(cover),* **warren lustro dull 80#/100#** *(cover, text)*
design/prepress **macintosh** *(quark xpress, adobe photoshop)*

This kit was used to reposition MTV to media buyers as a network of specific programs rather than 24 hours of music videos.

196 "DARE TO SEE IT" POSTER
production **steven newman**
design/prepress **macintosh** *(quark xpress, adobe illustrator)*

197 MEAD SHOW INVITATION
printer **lithographix, los angeles, california**
print run **2,000**
printing technique **five pms and matte varnish over three pms and varnish, white engraving, individually stitched**
paper stock **beckett enhance**
design/prepress **traditional and computer**
budget **$7,500** *(invitation package)*

The design identity created for the 1992 Mead Show sponsored by Butler Paper was adapted to the invitation, envelope, and reminder card, and the shopping bags were filled with paper promotions and samples at the show.

198 LET YOUR IMAGINATION SOAR
paper stock **neenah classic linen**
design/prepress **macintosh** *(adobe illustrator)*

Bright colors and flat ink coverage were used to show the printability of Linen paper. The poster demonstrates that the paper also embosses very well.

199 HEAD 1993-1994 GOLF EQUIPMENT CATALOG
printer **heritage press, dallas, texas**
print run **25,000**
printing technique **four-color process, one pms, and gloss/satin varnish**
design/prepress **macintosh quadra 950** *(quark xpress, adobe illustrator)*
budget **$120,000**

To create an attitude that is upbeat compared to the traditional golf company, the designers used color filters in the product photography and a nontraditional format.

200 NETWORK SALES KIT & COLLATERAL
production manager **will lampe**
printer **printcraft, minneapolis, minnesota**
print run **5,000**
printing technique **four-color process, embossing, liquid lamination, thermography**
paper stock **champion kromekote, french speckletone, warren lustro dull, neenah uv ultra, curtis flannel**
design/prepress **traditional and macintosh quadra 950**
budget **$50,000**

This package was designed to reposition Times Mirror Magazine Network as vibrant and energetic men's group. It combines imagery which projects strength with a conversational style of copywriting.

203 ETONIC PRODUCT CATALOG
copywriter **mike sheehan**
printer **daniels printing company, everett, massachussetts**
print run **12,000**
printing technique **four-color process and two waterless varnishes**
paper stock **quintessence** *(cover, text)*
design/prepress **traditional and macintosh** *(quark xpress)*
budget **$175,000**

With a focus on the high-tech running market, this catalog conveys a serious runner's tone without being emotionless.

204 MICROSOFT 1994 TECH-EDUCATION FLYERS
printer **graphic arts center, portland, oregon**
print run **100,000**
printing technique **four pms** *(cover),* **three-color** *(text page)*
paper stock **environment 80# text moonrock**
design/prepress **traditional and macintosh quadra 800** *(quark xpress)*

This direct mail piece to potential attendees of a Microsoft conference depicts the technical and global nature of the conference with visually impacting cover graphics and spreads.

205 LEO'S DANCEWEAR CATALOG
printer **lithotone**
print run **20,000**
printing technique **offset, tri-tone photos and special fifth color**
paper stock **warren loe dull**
design/prepress **traditional**
budget **$50,000**

206 *ARGUS POSTERS*
printer **the argus press, niles, illinois**
print run **1,500**
printing technique **6/6**
design/prepress **quadra 800**

207 *HANG TEN FOOTWEAR CATALOG/SPRING 1994*
printer **ross-ellis ltd., montreal, canada**
print run **10,000**
printing technique **full-color process and aqueous coating**
paper stock **200m supercoat, book stock**
design/prepress **macintosh centris 650** (quark xpress, adobe illustrator)
budget **$30,000**

This catalog combined the heritage of the licensed brand—Hang Ten—with a current trendy aesthetic and real-life models to communicate the attitude of the product.

208 *NMR SLIM JIM DIRECT MAIL*
production **steven newman**
printer **jds graphics, engelwood, new jersey**
print run **3,000**
design/prepress **macintosh** (quark xpress, adobe illustrator, adobe photoshop)

210 *THE CHASE MANHATTAN BANK CORPORATE GIFT CATALOG*
printer **thompson printing**
print run **7,500**
printing technique **four-color process and spot varnish on text**
paper stock **starwhite vicksburg 80#** (cover), **warren lustro gloss 100#** (text)
design/prepress **computer**
budget **$75,000**

211 *GET A GRIP*
printer **the emerson companies, cleveland, ohio**
paper stock **beckett concept 80#** (cover)

214 *WHERE ON EARTH CAN YOU USE BECKETT ENHANCE! MARBLE?*
printer **wendling printing co., newport, kentucky**
paper stock **beckett enhance!**

216 *POLYTRADE 15TH ANNIVERSARY PAPER SAMPLE BROCHURE*
copywriter **mark chan**
printer **printing force co., hong kong**
print run **1,500**
printing technique **16 color, offset**
design/prepress **traditional and macintosh fx** (adobe illustrator, adobe photoshop)
budget **$7,900**

217 *WQCD-FM, NYC PROMOTIONAL PRESSKIT*
production **steven newman**
printer **dicksons, atlanta, georgia**
print run **5,000**
design/prepress **traditional**

218 *PRINTING BY DESIGN*
printer **sidney printing works, cincinnati, ohio**
printing technique **die cuts, gradations, varnishes**
design/prepress **traditional and computer**

To showcase their printing abilities, Sidney Printing Works commisioned six design firms to create posters with a "cityscapes" theme which were then bound into a book.

221 *THE EVOLUTION OF AN IMAGE*
copywriter **alan adler**
computer graphics **john o'neill**
printer **anderson printing, los angeles, california**
print run **8,000**
printing technique **agfa cristalraster™ stochastic screening**
paper stock **potlach eloquence gloss 100#** (cover), **james river curtis parchment parchkin mottled basis 60**
design/prepress **macintosh iici** (adobe photoshop 2.5)
budget **all services pro bono**

This calendar was used as a sell-promotional piece for all involved.

222 *1991 BICYCLE & ACCESSORIES CATALOG*
production **rodney hines**
printer **anderson lithograph, los angeles, california**
print run **100,000**
paper stock **simpson evergreen gloss**
design/prepress **traditional and macintosh** (aldus pagemaker)

223 *DIRECT MIAL PRODUCT BROCHURES & CATALOG*
printer **welsh graphics**
print run **50,000**

224 *PERFORMANCE CO-OP BOOK*
printer **consolidated stoghton**
print run **5,000**
printing techique **offset**
design/prepress **traditional and computer** (quark xpress, adobe photoshop)
budget **$10,000**

DESIGN FIRMS

ADDISON CORPORATE ANNUAL REPORTS
79 fifth avenue
new york, ny 10003

AFTER HOURS CREATIVE
1201 east jefferson, suite 100-b
phoenix, az 85034

ALAN CHAN DESIGN COMPANY
2/f shiu lam building
23 luard road
wanchai, hong kong

ALEXANDER ISLEY DESIGN
361 broadway, suite 111
new york, ny 10013

BELK MIGNOGNA ASSOCIATES LTD.
381 park avenue south, suite 1401
new york, ny 10016

BJORNSON DESIGN ASSOCIATES INC.
153 north third street, second floor
philadelphia, pa 19106

BROOM & BROOM
360 post street, suite 1100
san francisco, ca 94108

CASTAGNE COMMUNICATIONS, INC.
11 west 42nd street, suite 3100
new york, ny 10036

CHERMAYEFF & GEISMAR
15 east 26th street
new york, ny 10010

CHRIS GORMAN ASSOCIATES, INC.
305 madison avenue
new york, ny 10165

CLARKE GOWARD
535 boylston street
boston, ma 02116

COOK AND SHANOSKY ASSOCIATES INC.
103 carnegie center, suite 203
princeton, nj 08540

COPELAND HIRTHLER DESIGN +
COMMUNICATION
40 inwood circle
atlanta, ga 30309

CORNING INC., CORPORATE DESIGN
DEPARTMENT
one riverfront plaza, mp-mq-e1-j14
corning, ny 14830

CORPORATE REPORTS INC.
6 lenox pointe
atlanta, ga 30324

D.Z. COMMUNICATIONS
11288 ventura boulevard, #727
studio city, ca 91604

DOUBLESPACE
170 fifth avenue
new york, ny 10010

DRENTTEL DOYLE PARTNERS
1123 broadway
new york, ny 10010

EARL GEE DESIGN
501 second street, suite 700
san francisco, ca 94107

EM2 DESIGN
530 means street, suite 402
atlanta, ga 30318

ESKIND WADDELL
260 richmond street west, suite 201
toronto, m5v 1w5, canada

FIORENTINO ASSOCIATES
134 west 26th street
new york, ny 10001

FRANKFURT BALKIND PARTNERS
(formerly frankfurt gips balkind)
244 east 58th street
new york, ny 10028

FRAZIER DESIGN
600 townsend street, suite 412w
san francisco, ca 94103

GARDNER + GRETEMAN
617 east wiliam
wichita, ks 67202

THE GRAPHIC EXPRESSION, INC.
330 east 59th street, fifth floor
new york, ny 10022

GREENFIELD/BELSER LTD.
1818 north street northwest, #110
washington, dc 20036

HERMAN MILLER, INC.
855 east main avenue
po box 302
zeeland, mi 49465

HORNALL ANDERSON DESIGN WORKS
1008 western, suite 600
seattle, wa 98104

HOUSTON EFFLER & PARTNERS
360 newbury street
boston, ma 02115

HOWRY DESIGN ASSOCIATES
120 montgomery street, #2140
san francisco, ca 94104

IMAGES DESIGN
1201 west peachtree street, suite 3630
atlanta, ga 30309

JANN CHURCH PARTNERS, INC.
110 newport center drive
newport beach, ca 92660

JENSEN DESIGN ASSOCIATES
324 east bixby road
long beach, ca 90807

JOHNSON & SIMPSON GRAPHIC DESIGNERS
49 bleeker street
newark, nj 07102

THE KOTTLER CALDERA GROUP
1201 east jefferson, a25
phoenix, az 85034

LEIMER CROSS DESIGN
140 lakeside avenue, #310
seattle, wa 98122

LISA LEVIN DESIGN
124 locust avenue
mill valley, ca 94941

LISKA AND ASSOCIATES, INC.
676 north st. clair, suite 1550
chicago, il 60611

LITTLE & COMPANY
1010 south seventh street
minneapolis, mn 55415

LOUEY/RUBINO DESIGN GROUP INC.
2525 main street, suite 204
santa monica, ca 90405

MAMOLITTI CHAN DESIGN
7/9 waxman parade
po box 109
west brunswick
victoria, australia 3055

MARK OLDACH DESIGN
3525 north oakley boulevard
chicago, il 60612

MAUCK + ASSOCIATES
303 locust street, suite 200
des moines, ia 50309

MAUREEN ERBE DESIGN
1948 south la cienega boulevard
los angeles, ca 90034

MC STUDIO/TIMES MIRROR MAGAZINES
2 park avenue
new york, ny 10016

MCDANIEL DESIGN INC.
29 schaefer road
maplewood, nj 07040

MENDELL & OBERER
widenmayerstr.12
d-80538 münchen, germany

MICHAEL MABRY DESIGN
212 sutter street
san francisco, ca 94108

MIDNIGHT OIL STUDIOS
51 melcher street
boston, ma 02210

MIKE QUON DESIGN OFFICE, INC.
568 broadway, suite 703
new york, ny 10012

MOBIUM
2000 the merchandise mart
200 world trade center
chicago, il 60654

MOHAWK PAPER MILLS
465 saratoga street
cahoes, ny 12047

MORLA DESIGN
463 bryant street
san francisco, ca 94107

NESNADNY & SCHWARTZ
10803 magnolia drive
cleveland, oh 44106

NICHOLAS ASSOCIATES
213 west institute place, suite 704
chicago, il 60610

NIKE DESIGN
one bowerman drive
beaverton, or 97005

NORTHLICH STOLLEY LAWARRE
LAMSON DESIGN
200 west fourth street
cincinnati, oh 45202

ODEN & ASSOCIATES
5140 wheelis drive
memphis, tn 38117

PENTAGRAM
212 fifth avenue
new york, ny 10010

PENTAGRAM DESIGN, INC.
620 davis
san francisco, ca 94111

PETRICK DESIGN
828 north wolcott avenue
chicago, il 60622

PLANET DESIGN COMPANY
229 state street
madison, wi 53703

PLATINUM
14 west 23rd street
new york, ny 10010

POLESE CLANCY
10 commercial wharf west
boston, ma 02110

RBMM/THE RICHARDS GROUP INC.
607 twin hills, suite 200
dallas, tx 75231

RUSSELL LEONG DESIGN
847 emerson street
palo alto, ca 94301

SAMATA ASSOCIATES
101 south first street
dundee, il 60118

SAYLES GRAPHIC DESIGN
308 eighth street
des moines, io 50309

SEGURA INC.
361 west chestnut street, first floor
chicago, il 60610

SIBLEY/PETEET DESIGN, INC.
965 slocum
dallas, tx 75207

SIEBERT DESIGN ASSOCIATES
1600 sycamore
cincinnati, oh 45210

SLAUGHTER/HANSON
2100 morris avenue
birmingham, al 35203

SPANGLER ASSOCIATES INC.
1110 third avenue, suite 800
seattle, wa 98101

TANAGRAM, INC.
855 west blackhawk
chicago, il 60622

THIEL VISUAL DESIGN
325 east chicago street
milwaukee, wi 53202

THIRST
855 west blackhawk street
chicago, il 60622

THOMAS RYAN DESIGN
po box 24449
nashville, tn 37202

TOMMY LI DESIGN LTD.
221 a, 5/f, wan chai road
hong kong

VAUGHN WEDEEN CREATIVE
407 rio grande northwest
albuquerque, nm 87104

WEYMOUTH DESIGN
332 congress street
boston, ma 02210

WHITE DESIGN
4510 east pacific coast highway,
suite 620
long beach, ca 90804

WINNER KOENIG & ASSOCIATES
777 south harbour island boulevard,
suite 190
tampa, fl 33602

WORKSIGHT
46 great jones street
new york, ny 10012

ZAHOR & BENDER INC.
200 east 33rd street
new york, ny 10066

CLIENTS

DESIGN FIRMS

CREATIVE DIRECTORS, ART DIRECTORS, DESIGNERS

ILLUSTRATORS

PHOTOGRAPHERS

Acknowledgements

My sincerest thanks to everyone who helped make this book possible. Special thanks to Mark Serchuck, Penny Sibal, Richard Liu, Susan Kapsis, Lorine Bamberg, Deby Harding, Francine Hornberger, Christine Brako, and Jami Hall at PBC International for all their assistance. Appreciation to Christine Woo for her research, encouragement and superb coaching. My colleagues at Mike Quon Design Office — especially John Steward for his invaluable design assistance and innovative layouts, Erick Kuo, Michael Ford, Andrew Jackson Kocher, Ron Edelstein, and Katherine Lumb. Thanks to Connie Silver, Henry Artis of the Art Directors Club of New York, and the many others I received advice from. I am grateful to all the designers, artists and photographers who contributed their splendid work for the publication. Finally, Katharine McAulay, for her patience, significant contributions, understanding and encouragement of this effort.

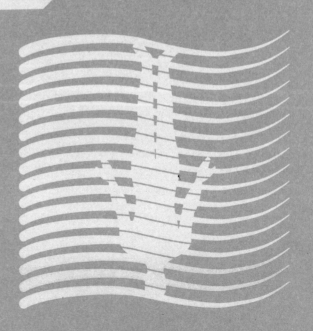